Comments on other *Amazing Stories* from readers & reviewers

"*Tightly written volumes filled with lots of wit and humour
about famous and infamous Canadians.*"
Eric Shackleton, *The Globe and Mail*

"*The heightened sense of drama and intrigue, combined with a
good dose of human interest is what sets* Amazing Stories *apart.*"
Pamela Klaffke, *Calgary Herald*

"*This is popular history as it should be... For this price,
buy two and give one to a friend.*"
Terry Cook, a reader from Ottawa, on **Rebel Women**

"*Glasner creates the moment of the explosion itself in
graphic detail...she builds detail upon gruesome detail
to create a convincingly authentic picture.*"
Peggy McKinnon, *The Sunday Herald*, on **The Halifax Explosion**

"*It was wonderful...I found I could not put it down.
I was sorry when it was completed.*"
Dorothy F. from Manitoba on **Marie-Anne Lagimodière**

"*Stories are rich in description, and bristle
with a clever, stylish realness.*"
Mark Weber, *Central Alberta Advisor*, on **Ghost Town Stories II**

"*A compelling read. Bertin...has selected only the most intriguing
tales, which she narrates with a wealth of detail.*"
Joyce Glasner, *New Brunswick Reader*, on **Strange Events**

"*The resulting book is one readers will want to share
with all the women in their lives.*"
Lynn Martel, *Rocky Mountain Outlook*, on **Women Explorers**

# THE BATTLE OF SEVEN OAKS

# THE BATTLE OF SEVEN OAKS

### And the Violent Birth of the Red River Settlement

*Nov. 2005*

*Best wishes*

*Irene*

**HISTORY**

## by Irene Ternier Gordon

PUBLISHED BY ALTITUDE PUBLISHING CANADA LTD.
1500 Railway Avenue, Canmore, Alberta  T1W 1P6
www.altitudepublishing.com
1-800-957-6888

Extreme care has been taken to ensure that all information presented in
this book is accurate and up to date. Neither the author nor the
publisher can be held responsible for any errors.

| Publisher | Stephen Hutchings |
| Associate Publisher | Kara Turner |
| Series Editor | Jill Foran |
| Editor | Lori Burwash |

We acknowledge the financial support of the Government
of Canada through the Book Publishing Industry Development
Program (BPIDP) for our publishing activities.

**Altitude GreenTree Program**
Altitude Publishing will plant twice as many trees as were used
in the manufacturing of this product.

**National Library of Canada Cataloguing in Publication Data**

Gordon, Irene Ternier
The Battle of Seven Oaks / Irene Gordon.

(Amazing stories)
ISBN 1-55439-025-7

1. Seven Oaks, Battle of, Winnipeg, Man., 1816. I. Title. II. Series: Amazing stories (Calgary, Alta.)

FC3212.4.G67 2005          971.27'01          C2005-902838-6

An application for the trademark for Amazing Stories™
has been made and the registered trademark is pending.

Printed and bound in Canada by Friesens
2 4 6 8 9 7 5 3 1

To the descendants of everyone involved in the events at Seven Oaks — Selkirk settlers, Métis and First Nations people, Nor'Wester and Hudson's Bay traders, and French-Canadian freemen — and most especially, to my grandson Felix. Felix, through his maternal grandmother, is a direct descendant of William McGillivray and his wife Susan.

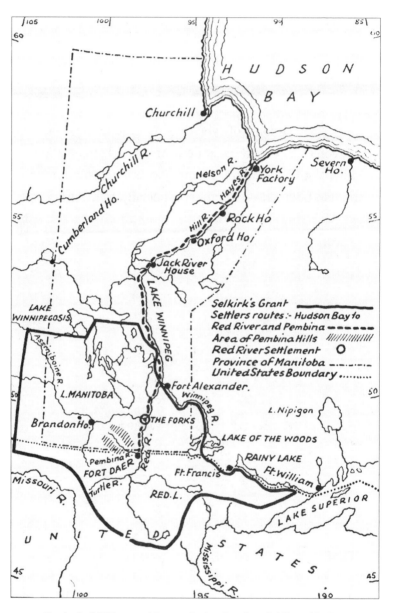

Map showing Selkirk's grant and the route taken by early settlers to Red River and Fort Daer

# Contents

# Prologue

*The lookout in the watchtower at Fort Douglas gave the alarm as soon as he caught the first indistinct sight of a party of horsemen riding across the plains that June afternoon. Governor Semple hurried into the tower and watched the riders through a spyglass for some minutes. Certain they were Métis, he called for 15 or 20 volunteers to go out and meet them. He waited impatiently while the men were issued weapons — muskets, bayonets, balls, and powder — but refused to take the three-pounder field piece (cannon), saying he was only going to see what the Métis wanted, not fight with them.*

*In the meantime, the Métis, led by Cuthbert Grant, came across three settlers working in a field and took them prisoner so they could not raise the alarm. Then, seeing Semple and his men marching towards them, Grant ordered a small advance party to make camp while he and the main party rode back to meet Semple.*

*The two groups halted when they came within hailing distance of each other. Grant ordered his men to fan out in a half-moon shape around Semple's men, who extended their line and retreated a few steps. Then they faced each other silently and motionlessly — Grant's men on horseback, Semple's on foot.*

*Grant gave an order to one of his men, François Fermin Boucher: "Tell Semple to surrender, or we will fire upon him." Boucher rode up to Semple, and the two men spoke briefly. Then Semple lost his temper. He seized the reins of Boucher's horse and may have grabbed at his gun. A second later a shot rang out.*

# Chapter 1
# The Largest Landowner in the World

**The Forks, September 1812**

A cannon blast shattered the noonday peace at The Forks one fine, late-summer day. The handful of Native people and French-Canadian freemen who were within earshot quickly gathered to see what was going on. Two Hudson's Bay men and three North West Company officers also appeared, but the Nor'West employees had to watch the proceedings from the opposite bank of the river because their officers had forbidden them to cross over from their post at Fort Gibraltar. There had been an uneasy relationship between the two rival fur trading companies in the area, HBC and NWC, for some years.

It was Captain Miles Macdonell who had fired the cannon. He had arrived at The Forks several days earlier (on August 30, 1812) with a group of 23 Scottish and Irish labourers who had made the 13-month trip from Scotland. Macdonell raised the Union Jack, flanked by his men, who formed a guard of honour. He then read two official documents that would be of great importance to the future of the region.

The first was a patent conveying almost 187,000 square kilometres of territory centred on the junction of the Red and Assiniboine Rivers (long known as The Forks) to a Scottish nobleman named Thomas Douglas, the Fifth Earl of Selkirk. The second document gave Macdonell authority, as governor of the territory, to take possession in Selkirk's name.

Selkirk had plans to settle impoverished Scottish and Irish families on this land, which was to be known as Assiniboia. Macdonell and his men were an advance party, assigned the task of making preparations for the first group of settlers, who were expected to arrive before winter.

All told, Assiniboia, which formed a natural basin, covered an area about the size of England, Scotland, and Ireland combined. When Selkirk received this land grant, he became the largest landowner in the world. The western border of Assiniboia was in line with the head of the Assiniboine River (located in what is now eastern Saskatchewan), and it extended almost to Lake Superior in the east. From south to north, Selkirk's grant stretched from northern Minnesota and North Dakota to the southern parts of lakes Winnipeg and Winnipegosis.

Macdonell described the country in a letter to Selkirk: "The country exceeds any idea I had formed of its goodness.

Miles Macdonell

I am only astonished it has lain so long unsettled. With good management, buffalo in winter and fish in summer are sufficient to subsist any number of people." Macdonell, who found the soil fertile and the climate "most extraordinarily healthy," observed that fever and ague, "so prevalent in other parts of America," were unknown.

Macdonell also reported to Selkirk that he had all available artillery fired following the reading of the patents, and that the assembled crowd gave three cheers. Then, he added, "the gentlemen met at my tent and a keg of spirits was turned out for the people." Macdonell used the term "gentlemen" to refer to himself and the HBC and Nor'West officers. "People" referred to everyone else.

At this time there was no permanent community at the junction of the Red and Assiniboine Rivers, now the centre of the city of Winnipeg. A handful of Nor'West fur traders were manning the recently constructed Fort Gibraltar. Two employees of the rival Hudson's Bay Company also happened to be camping in the area when the Macdonell party arrived, but the HBC had no buildings there. A few French-Canadian trappers and buffalo hunters lived with their Métis families in rough log cabins nearby, when they were not out hunting on the plains. These hunters were known as "freemen," because they were not under contract to either of the two fur trade companies.

Until the arrival of Macdonell and his party, the only agriculture in the area consisted of gardens planted by the factors in charge of some of the trading posts. Most of the freemen had been raised on farms in Quebec, and some of the English and Scottish-born fur traders had come from farm backgrounds, but agriculture was unknown to the Native peoples of the immediate area until the Europeans arrived.

Macdonell and his men set up a temporary camp across the river from Fort Gibraltar. Two of Macdonell's relatives — his brother John and his cousin Alexander Macdonell — were Nor'Westers who happened to be at Fort Gibraltar when Miles arrived. Although the Nor'Westers were hostile to the idea of settlement, they greeted Miles hospitably and invited him and the two HBC men to dinner. Miles wrote in his journal that he "passed a very pleasant evening and only returned at 1 in the morning."

# Chapter 2
# Plans of a Grand Colonizer

**Scotland, 1771–1811**

On June 20, 1771, workers and tenants of the estate of the fourth Earl of Selkirk were celebrating the birth of the Earl's seventh son. A visitor observed that with six older brothers, the newborn Thomas Douglas would have no chance of inheriting either the Selkirk title or the family fortune. "Gawd mon," the visitor said to one of the servants, "ye'd think ye'd faithered the bairn yoursel. Why all the hilarity? This is not ev'n the furst."

Unlikely as it seems, the visitor was wrong. One by one, Thomas's older brothers all died of fever or in battle. Finally, in 1799, his father died, and Thomas became the fifth Earl of Selkirk at the age of 28. He now had the money to carry out his dream of establishing agricultural settlements in British

North America for some of the destitute people of Ireland and the Scottish Highlands.

After reading *Voyages* by well-known explorer and Nor'West trader Alexander Mackenzie, Selkirk decided the Red River would be an ideal location for a settlement. In 1802 he had written to the British Colonial Secretary extolling the climate and fertility of the area around Lake Winnipeg. "Here, therefore, the colonists may, with moderate exertion of industry, be certain of a comfortable subsistence, and they may also raise some valuable objects of exportation."

The response from the colonial office was not enthusiastic, as Britain did not favour the emigration of its citizens. Nonetheless, Selkirk went ahead with his plans, even though at this time the only way to obtain land for settlement was for a wealthy person to purchase land from the Crown and be responsible for placing suitable settlers on it. The settlers, in turn, purchased the land from the new owner. Selkirk settled 800 Scottish Highlanders in Prince Edward Island in 1803 and made an unsuccessful attempt the following year to establish a settlement in Upper Canada.

In 1807 Selkirk married Jean Wedderburn-Colvile, whose brother Andrew was an influential member of the governing body of the Hudson's Bay Company. The HBC controlled the vast area of North America known as Rupert's Land, including the Red River. To the east of Rupert's Land were the separate British colonies of Upper and Lower Canada (parts of today's Ontario and Quebec), Prince Edward Island, Nova Scotia,

Lord Selkirk

New Brunswick and Newfoundland. Canada would not come into existence as a country for another 60 years.

Selkirk bought up HBC shares in hopes that the governing body would agree to provide him with land for a settlement at the Red River. On February 26, 1811, the HBC Committee passed a motion that "Wedderburn-Colvile be desired to request Lord Selkirk to lay before the Committee the terms on which he will accept a grant of land within the territories of the Company."

In June 1811, Selkirk's offer was accepted by a majority

of stockholders representing stocks valued at almost £30,000 (an amount having approximately the same purchasing power as $2.5 million Canadian in 2002). A substantial — and outraged — minority of stockholders were opposed to the deal. They were North West Company men such as Alexander Mackenzie, who had been quietly buying up shares at the same time as Selkirk was. The minority stockholders delivered a formal written protest outlining the "grounds and reasons" for their objections. They charged that Selkirk held a controlling number of stocks and voted himself the land grant, but HBC minutes show that this was untrue. Selkirk only held stock to the value of £4,087 at this time. However, by January 1812 (within six months of his receiving the land grant), Selkirk had bought over £18,000 worth of stocks.

The minority stockholders also argued that, if the land was to be sold, it should have been offered to the general public, not given to Selkirk for a token payment of 10 shillings. As well, they said, Selkirk offered no assurance that he would ever establish a settlement or produce any benefits to the HBC. He might simply be trying to enrich himself at the expense of the stockholders. Finally, and most importantly in the Nor'Westers' view, "it has been found that colonization is at all times unfavourable to the fur trade."

The vote of the majority prevailed, and the grant was officially conveyed to Selkirk, "his heirs and assigns for ever." The deed stated that one-tenth of the land should be made available to men who had been employed by the HBC for at least three years. Such men, depending on their rank in the company, would be eligible for land grants of between 200 and 1,000 acres. They were to receive these grants on condition that they or their assigns become settlers and cultivate the land. Selkirk was required to settle at least 1,000 families at the Red River within 10 years. The deed stated that Selkirk was not to compete with the HBC's fur trade, but he could ship any other produce from the settlement to the Port of London by way of Hudson Bay.

Selkirk also made an agreement with the prospective settlers. For £10 sterling per head, a settler would receive transportation, 100 acres of land at five shillings per acre, and one year's provisions. The HBC would provide markets for surplus farm products, and the settlement would have schools, mills, roads, and bridges, as well as a Presbyterian church with a Gaelic-speaking minister.

The HBC later justified to the colonial minister its acceptance of Selkirk's offer. The main argument was that settlers would be a source of "a certain supply of provisions at a moderate price" to help feed fur trade employees, as it was too expensive to import provisions from England. The company also expected that it would gain "considerable eventual benefit from the improvement of their landed property by means of agricultural settlements."

Anxious to begin settlement immediately, Selkirk asked Miles Macdonell, a 45-year-old farmer and military man, to serve as governor of the settlement. Selkirk had first met

Macdonell in 1804 in Upper Canada and thought he was "very much of a gentleman in manners and sentiment." Selkirk was impressed that Macdonell, whose family had immigrated to New York from Scotland and then moved on to Upper Canada after the American Revolution, had cleared "a considerable tract" of land and was building a good house and a large barn. Selkirk noted in his diary that Macdonell also "proposes to clear on about 100 acres more — laying down to grass as soon as cleared — to keep a little tillage and a considerable stock of cattle which he reckons more profitable."

Macdonell was also a lieutenant in the Royal Canadian Volunteer Regiment. He had served at Fort George (Niagara-on-the-Lake) from 1800 until his regiment was disbanded in 1802.

However, Macdonell was frequently in debt. In 1804 he wrote, "Mere farming will hardly support my family in the manner I would wish." Between 1802 and 1811, he wrote numerous letters trying to secure a new military position, but without success. Many people found Macdonell arrogant and vain, and he had difficulty winning the loyalty and trust of the men in his charge. So he was delighted to accept Selkirk's offer.

Selkirk had hoped to recruit 200 men for his advance party, mostly to work at Hudson's Bay posts, but also about 30 to prepare for the arrival of the settlers and their families.

Upon seeing Selkirk's newspaper advertisement for people to immigrate to Hudson Bay, Simon McGillivray, whose brother William was head of the North West Company, wrote a letter against settlement to the *Inverness Journal* (June 21, 1811). He said that Selkirk's advertisement spoke of settlements being already formed "where none exist and where it is impossible, from the nature of the country and the severity of the climate, that settlement ever can be established." The advertisement, he said, "asserts a positive falsehood in ascribing the climate to be the same as that of Canada."

He also noted that the proposed settlement was a long way from Hudson Bay, where the settlers would first make landfall following their voyage from Scotland. They would still face a difficult journey on rivers with strong currents, dangerous rapids, and numerous portages. McGillivray said the distance was nearly 2,000 miles (3,200 kilometres), but it is actually closer to 1,000 miles (1,600 kilometres). He argued that it would be difficult or impossible for the settlers to reach the proposed site of the settlement before freeze-up. "It is my firm belief," he wrote, "that many of them will perish before spring, from excessive cold and from want of food, if a sufficient supply of provisions is not shipped with them."

Finally, McGillivray warned that even if they safely reached the intended settlement site, the settlers would be 3,200 kilometres from the sea or any other settlement of European people. They would also be surrounded by warlike nations who would consider them intruders and would destroy their homes, crops, and cattle.

Macdonell and his party were to sail from Stornoway, a

port in the Scottish Hebrides, where, Macdonell said, the collector of customs "became a genius in finding technicalities which would delay departure." Selkirk's fellow stockholder and a strong opponent of this venture, Alexander Mackenzie, had been born near Stornoway, and his aunt was married to the Stornoway collector of customs.

Macdonell finally sailed in late July 1811, at least a month later than normal for voyages to Hudson Bay, and with only 105 men instead of the 200 he had hoped for. To make matters worse, strong head winds extended the voyage to 61 days, the longest crossing on record.

# Chapter 3
# Difficult Beginnings

**York Factory, 1811–1812**

It was September 24, 1811 before the ship finally reached York Factory at the south end of Hudson Bay. By this time — proving Simon McGillivray correct — ice was already forming on the river. It was obvious that the Macdonell party would not be able to reach the Red River before freeze-up.

William Auld, superintendent of the HBC's Northern Department, was at York Factory when Macdonell arrived. The two men greeted each other civilly, but took an immediate dislike to each other. Auld strongly opposed the new style of HBC management implemented in 1810, with its severe cost-cutting measures. He argued that the new policies were preventing the HBC from more effectively competing with the NWC — something that required both more trade goods and more personnel, rather than cutbacks. He also strongly opposed settlement at the Red River.

Macdonell and the 23 men who formed his advance party soon set up camp about 13 kilometres away from York Factory, on the north side of the Nelson River. They built rough log cabins roofed with poles covered with sods and constructed crude stone fireplaces for heat and cooking. Thinly scraped rawhide in the windows provided a meagre light.

Neither Auld nor Macdonell was blameless in the dispute that raged between them over the winter. Auld wrote of Macdonell, "If Lord Selkirk had advertised for a fool of the first magnitude, he never could have better succeeded than he has done with the present man. He disgusted every one of the settlers and servants ... He has encouraged the Canadian traders to treat him with contempt by his childish partiality."

As well, Macdonell was disappointed in the calibre of his men. None of them had ever used a gun before, and all were equally inexperienced with axes. Macdonell's bad temper and quickness to display his authority only made the problems worse. He soon lost control of the men, and they grew restless and quarrelsome over the long winter because they had little to keep them occupied. About the only thing these Scottish Presbyterians and Irish Catholics agreed on was their dislike of Macdonell. Almost everyone who could write, it seemed, wrote to Selkirk to complain.

Macdonell's party relied on York Factory for provisions other than fresh meat. Auld warned them of the dangers of scurvy and promised to send them cranberries and crystallized lemon juice. Before these arrived, though, scurvy had already broken out, and the men were forced to treat themselves by drinking spruce tea. On January 21, Macdonell acknowledged that Auld had delivered supplies, including peas, oatmeal, flour, essence of malt, cranberries, and a keg of barley. However, the barley was part of the supply meant for planting in the new settlement and was not to be eaten. Because of an abundance of wild game, especially deer, there was sufficient food, but the diet was limited and monotonous.

## Journey to the Red River, Summer 1812

Finally on July 6, 1812, the river was free of ice, and Macdonell and his men were able to complete their trip to the Red River via the Hayes River and Lake Winnipeg. The first leg was the 250 kilometres upstream from York Factory to Jack River Post (now called Norway House) on Playgreen Lake at the north end of Lake Winnipeg. The land rose more than 200 metres over that distance, so it was necessary to carry cargoes and sometimes the boats themselves over 34 portages. From Jack River, it was another 185 kilometres across Lake Winnipeg and up the Red River to The Forks.

For travel by water, the Nor'Westers exclusively used birchbark canoes, which were light enough to carry over the portages. The HBC traders, on the other hand, usually travelled in heavy York boats that they had to pull over portages on log rollers. York boats, constructed of overlapping wood planks, typically had 8.5-metre keels but were about 11 metres long from stem to stern, as each end extended out from the keel. The pointed ends made it easier to push the boat off a rock or a shoal. Each boat had a crew of six or eight oarsmen, a steersman, and sometimes a bowman.

On reaching the Red River at the south end of Lake Winnipeg, the men were relieved to find that it was not the colour of blood and that no shots were fired at them. Nor'Westers back home had hinted that hostile Natives would shoot at them from the shadows and that the river had received its name from the blood thus spilled.

The land immediately south of the lake was quite swampy. One traveller at that time said the middle one of the three channels by which the Red River empties into Lake Winnipeg had "a tolerable good encampment at its mouth." Elsewhere, the low river banks were made of black mud that "form'd into a kind of mortar that adheres to the foot like tar, so that at every step we raise several pounds of mud."

There were numerous wild fowl and fish — along with lots of mosquitoes. The river was quite deep, with a gentle current. The group finally reached some rapids (in the present-day Lockport area). There, the river banks became steeper, and the newcomers had their first sight of the flat, treeless prairie or grassland stretching into the distance. They saw large animals such as deer, bears, and wolves, and a few buffalo cows grazing with their young on the rich grass. The prairie looked rich and peaceful in the late August sunshine.

## The Forks and Pembina, Fall 1812

Once the newcomers had set up camp at The Forks, mosquitoes and common garter snakes were the worst nuisances they faced. The snakes, they learned, lurked in the many graves found nearby — the result of a smallpox epidemic in the area some 30 years previous. Although the snakes were harmless, the men were disconcerted to find them in the bedrolls.

The group was surprised to learn that the HBC had not built any shelters, and there was no food supply ready. Macdonell wrote angrily to Selkirk, "Notwithstanding all the orders The Company posts in this quarter might have had to provide for our arrival, there was not one bag of pemmican or any other article of provisions reserved for us." There may have been a shortage of workers, but undoubtedly the main reason for not carrying out these orders was a lack of enthusiasm for the idea of settlement.

Macdonell selected a site for the permanent settlement just north of The Forks. This area, which he named Point Douglas, was almost clear of trees and brush due to a fire some years previous. He began constructing a temporary storehouse almost immediately. Only two days later, he impatiently wrote in his journal, "Set my men about cutting and carrying timber for the store, they make very slow progress."

He set five men to work building a rough shelter, cultivating the ground to seed winter wheat, and cutting and stacking prairie grass for the livestock. Then he left with the rest of his men for Pembina, about 100 kilometres south of The Forks, to make preparations for the settlers to spend the winter there. Both the HBC and the Nor'Westers already had forts at Pembina. More importantly, Pembina was closer to the buffalo herds, which would be their main source of food over the winter. Huge herds of buffalo had roamed around The Forks when LaVerendrye arrived there in 1738, but by 1810, few buffalo were left in the area, and hunters had to follow the herds south or westward.

At Pembina, Macdonell chose a site for a winter fort and left his men cutting logs to build it — except for one, whose job it was to fish with a bent nail to provide food for the woodcutters. Macdonell then returned to The Forks, taking back with him two horses, a harrow, and a supply of buffalo meat. The settlers had only spades and hoes to cultivate the soil before they planted the grain by hand-broadcasting it. Someone finally made a rough plough, but it was poorly made, as none of the settlers was a skilled blacksmith.

On October 13, Macdonell wrote that he had engaged a freeman named DeLorme "to treat with the Indians, assist and direct my people in building." He had also hired a Métis labourer and a hunter. He planned to leave only five men at The Forks for the winter and to "deposit all my seed grain, liquor, and ammunition in the NWC fort for security."

The second party of Selkirk settlers, led by Irishman Owen Keveny, arrived at York Factory on September 6, 1812, about a week after Macdonell's group arrived at the Red

River. Like Macdonell, Keveny had leadership problems. During the trip, some of the settlers accused him of treating them "with tyranny." Keveny defended his harshness as necessary against agitators whose actions "were more heinous than insubordination." He neglected to explain what the "agitators" had done.

Keveny's group of settlers included 18 women and 11 children, and two days before the ship came to anchor their number increased by one. Young Mrs. Hugh McLean (first name unknown) gave birth to a daughter in the hold of the storm-tossed boat — surrounded by sacks of seed grain, a bin of oatmeal, and a small herd of sheep. The older women offered what comfort and assistance they could. Keveny reported the birth of the newest settler to Selkirk upon anchoring. He wrote that both mother and child were doing well and "tomorrow will be ready to proceed inland."

Immediately upon the ship's arrival at York Factory, the first wedding of Selkirk settlers took place. Although the couple were both Scotch Presbyterians, the ceremony was performed by an Irish Catholic priest who had arrived the previous year and was now returning to Ireland. The groom, James Fraser, was a Lowlander who spoke only English and the bride, Anne Bannerman, was a Highlander who spoke only Gaelic.

Many years later, according to family lore, a young girl asked Anne Fraser how she knew what Mr. Fraser meant when he told her he loved her and wanted her to be his wife.

Mrs. Fraser's response: "Wait until your own time comes, my dear, and you will know how."

When the Keveny settlers passed through Oxford House on their way to the Red River, factor William Sinclair replenished their food stocks and presented them with a bull and a heifer, which they named Adam and Eve. Sinclair had arrived in Rupert's Land from the Orkney Islands to work for the HBC in 1792. He built Oxford House in 1798 and lived there until 1814. He ordered seeds from Britain, and planted a garden and some grain. He also had some cattle shipped from the Orkney Islands and was able to establish a small dairy.

Sinclair was worried about the fate of the settlers because there were so many women and children in the group. He was also concerned about what he saw as the incompetence or inexperience of the men. In his report to HBC superintendent Auld he wrote, "I never saw such a number of helpless creatures in my life. They were so lazy and inactive that they have entirely disgusted the old hands."

The Keveny settlers arrived at The Forks in late October. They had a Highland piper in their party who stepped from the lead boat and piped them ashore. They offered a prayer of thanksgiving and were then greeted by Miles Macdonell with a salute from the swivel guns and a drink of rum.

The young single women were welcomed with immediate marriage proposals. The sister of one bride later wrote, "We had not been at Point Douglas for more than 24 hours before men flocked in, each eager to get a wife. On finding a maiden that suited their fancy, they would open negotiations at once; either with her or her parents."

One of these brides was asked by a descendant, "Weren't you afraid to marry in such a fashion a man whom you'd never seen before?" Her reply: "I just took a good look at him out of the corner of my eye as we stood to be 'kirked' [married] and I said to myself, 'I guess he'll do.' And time proved that he 'did' very well."

Because there were no clergymen in the settlement, Macdonell performed the marriage ceremonies. As he reported to Selkirk, "The young men and maids were not altogether idle in the matrimonial affairs. Many could hardly wait for your Captain to join them in that humble embrace."

Within a few days, the settlers were sent on to Pembina for the winter. They walked most of the way, arriving there on October 27, with the flag flying and their piper leading them. Macdonell hired two of the best known buffalo hunters, Jean-Baptiste Lagimodière and Peter Pangman, to provide food for the settlers over the winter. Pangman's nickname was "Bostonnais" because his father had come from New England. Lagimodière, born in Quebec, was the husband of Marie-Anne Gaboury, the first non-Native woman to reside permanently in the Red River community. She had arrived as a bride at Pembina in the summer of 1806.

On December 24, 1812, the flag was raised on the settlers' winter home at Pembina, which was named Fort Daer in honour of Selkirk's son.

# Chapter 4
# The First Year in the New Land

**Point Douglas and Fort Daer, 1812–1813**

During the winter of 1812–1813, food was scarce, the weather was much colder than the settlers were used to back home in Scotland and Ireland, and there was little to do to break the monotony. They may also have felt neglected, as Miles Macdonell spent much of his time in the company of the NWC officers.

The highlight of a dismal winter was a visit from William Sinclair, the factor of Oxford House, who trekked all the way to Fort Daer in mid-winter to check on them. Macdonell wrote in his journal, "Assembled our people. Mr. Sinclair asks for a holiday for them, and also liquor for them to drink. The people enjoyed themselves much and kept it up for the greater part of the night. The gentlemen did the same."

Owen Keveny was to remain in the settlement as second-in-command as long as Macdonell wished, but each complained about the other to Selkirk. Macdonell said Keveny was "distant and reserved" and "extremely unpopular among the people on account of his discipline." Keveny, in turn, said he had received "treatment which has given me disgust" from Macdonell. Selkirk reprimanded Macdonell, expressing dismay that Keveny, a man of great ability, had been "so completely thrown aside and employed to no useful purpose."

Nor were the earlier good relations between cousins Miles and Alexander Macdonell to last. In April 1813, Miles accused Alexander of "insidious and treacherous conduct during the winter in endeavouring to swerve my people from their duty," and he ordered the settlers to end all interaction with the Nor'Westers.

This dispute between the cousins seems to have arisen after Miles spoke with Hector McDonald, the indentured servant of another settler. McDonald, who regularly visited Alexander Macdonell to give him bagpipe lessons, testified before Miles Macdonell on March 24 that Alexander had tried to convince him to go to Canada and had offered to transport him there in the spring. Also, McDonald said, Alexander had asked him many questions about what was going on at Fort Daer. If McDonald admitted that provisions were scarce, Alexander would remark that "if they should be a day or two without provisions it was sufficient to break all engagements, and the men had a right to go where they pleased."

Finally one evening, Alexander told McDonald that he should "hold himself in readiness" and tell everyone that he intended to go away with the Indians. At the same time, he was to keep secret everything Alexander had said.

Another Nor'West officer later told McDonald that the Nor'Westers could not have taken any of the settlers away that spring because they didn't have enough provisions. He went on to suggest, however, that if 20 of the colonists joined together in the summer, they might take a boat away from Captain Miles Macdonell by force. The officer said that, if they did so, he would make the road clear for them once they reached the mouth of the Winnipeg River.

Spring finally arrived. On May 3, 1813, Miles Macdonell baptized a baby daughter born to Hector and Margaret McDonald. Then in mid-May the settlers began returning to The Forks. Owen Keveny went to Brandon House, an HBC post located near the junction of the Assiniboine and Souris Rivers, to procure pemmican for the settlers. After delivering the pemmican to The Forks, Keveny left for York Factory.

At the end of May, Peter Fidler, a fur trader and surveyor who was in charge of Brandon House, spent a few days at the Red River surveying the new settlement, using the river lot system of Lower Canada. He divided Point Douglas into seven small lots and surveyed 100-acre farm lots along the west bank of the Red River extending north from Point Douglas. Each farm had a 10-chain (200 metre) river frontage and extended at right angles to the river for two miles (3200 metres), with an additional two miles as hay privilege.

Fidler had married his Cree wife Mary *à la façon du pays* (literally "in the way of the country") in 1794, and they had 14 children. He carefully noted the arrival of each child in a notebook. The first entry indicated that Tom was born at York Factory at 12:08 a.m. on June 20, 1795. The final entry was for Harriet, born at 4:53 on July 9, 1822.

Miles Macdonell, like a number of his contemporaries, was strongly critical of marriages *à la façon du pays*, even when they were as long-lasting and affectionate as Fidler's. Because of this, Macdonell objected to Fidler's appointment as permanent surveyor for the settlement. He wrote to Selkirk suggesting that in order to curb such marriages, the HBC should allow its servants to bring wives from Scotland or England.

On May 18, 1813, Miles Macdonell wrote in his journal that John McLeod and Bostonnais Pangman, who were in charge of HBC affairs at The Forks for the summer, were building a fort on the orders of their immediate superior, Hugh Heney. Macdonell was not pleased about this and wrote a letter of complaint to Selkirk on July 17, 1813. "Mr. Heney has established a trading post close by us here, I believe purposely to annoy us and in direct opposition to his chief, Mr. Hillier, who had ordered men to be left at Pembina and not the forks of the Red and Assiniboine rivers. It brings the Indians to camp too near."

The construction that Miles Macdonell had arranged

for in the settlement over the previous fall and winter was not completed — perhaps because of the severe weather or the workers' sheer incompetence. At any rate, the settlers were forced to live in tents for most of the summer.

Macdonell immediately hired new workers, and he chronicled the preparations for construction in his journal over the next few weeks. Typical entries: June 4, "Engaged 3 Canadians for house building." June 7, "Engaged 2 more Canadians for jobwork to get pickets for the garden." June 30, "The Canadians have prepared timber for a house 54 feet long. Have removed (the timber) to this side the river. A party is sent to bring over the foundation sills." July 2, "The Canadians bring across the whole of the house timber." July 3, "Traced on the ground the site of the house and put posts at the extreme angles of the proposed fort."

The winter wheat sown in the fall of 1812 — along with the wheat, peas, rye, hemp, barley, and corn sown in the spring of 1813 — was almost a complete failure. The oats were late and froze. Only the potatoes yielded well. Macdonell reported to Selkirk that the crop failure resulted from bad seed, drought after sowing, grubs, and faulty cultivation.

What little grain the settlers had was ground into flour between two round flat stones known as a "quern." A handle fixed to the upper stone was used to turn it upon the lower stone. The settlers also learned from the local people how to use native foods and plants. Red willow furnished a tobacco substitute known as *kinikinik* and was also used as a poultice against swelling. The inner bark of the poplar, which tasted somewhat like grapefruit, made a good spring tonic. Pemmican, while often eaten "as is," was sometimes cooked in a stew called "rubaboo," with potatoes and any other available vegetables. Another pemmican dish was prepared by mixing shredded pemmican with flour and water and then frying it.

There are only sketchy reports about how many livestock the settlers had in the earliest days. They may have had four cows, two bulls, pigs, some poultry, and a team of horses. The young bull and cow obtained at Oxford House apparently became quite adept at getting in and out of the boat at portages during their trip to The Forks. Fidler may also have purchased a bull, a cow, and a yearling heifer from the Nor'Westers at Fort La Souris, across from the HBC's Brandon House.

Selkirk sent a flock of 21 very valuable, golden-fleeced Merino sheep from Spain along with the Keveny settlers. He had decided that high-quality wool could be shipped economically from the Red River to British woollen mills in 90-pound bales, and common Scottish Blackface sheep would not do for this purpose. All except one of the Merino sheep arrived safely at The Forks, but one ewe and two of the four rams died over the winter. Insufficient feed and hungry dogs meant that before long the Merino sheep were extinct. The settlers continued to raise common sheep, however, and most of their clothing was knit from homespun wool. It is said that the women knitted during virtually every waking minute when their hands were not occupied with other work.

Fish, including whitefish, goldeye, sturgeon, and catfish, were an important part of the settlers' diet. Large quantities of fish were dried for winter use. Sturgeon or catfish oil was also sprinkled on fleeces to soften the fibres, worked into hides to soften them, and later used to oil gears in mills or farm machinery. In the earliest days of settlement, fish oil or buffalo tallow was used for lighting. A piece of rag dipped into a small container of oil formed a crude lamp. Candles made from buffalo tallow were more commonly used later on.

At first the cooking was done over open fireplaces. A bit later, people used oblong metal box stoves that the HBC imported from Scotland because they could be dismantled and shipped flat. Most homes also had outdoor clay ovens for baking. The few settlers who had a bit of spare money or goods to trade could buy things such as tea, coffee, sugar, rice, currants, and raisins from the HBC, but such things were luxuries for most people in the early years.

Entertainment was limited. Macdonell wrote to Selkirk that on Christmas Day the settlers had played hurl (a game similar to hockey) against the fur traders on the river. On another occasion, Macdonell wrote that he had given "a dance to the bagpipe this evening to the people — very pleasant party. The gentlemen, men, and women enjoyed themselves and encroached on the Sabbath." The older

Presbyterians were not pleased, as they strongly disapproved of dancing, especially on the Sabbath.

### Fort Churchill, 1813

A party of 94 settlers from Kildonan, Scotland, began their trip to the Red River in June 1813 aboard the ship *Prince of Wales.* They felt privileged, as over 700 people had applied to make the journey, but the Nor'Westers had leased most of the available ships in order to block Selkirk's plans. This voyage was dogged with misfortune from the beginning. The badly overcrowded and poorly crewed ship ran into bad weather. Worst of all, an outbreak of typhus during the voyage killed a number of people, including the settlers' popular leader, a medical doctor named Peter Laserre.

The ship's captain, anxious to get rid of his infected passengers, refused to take them to York Factory and instead dropped them off at Fort Churchill. Furthermore, the ship's crew did not unload all of the settlers' belongings, and some of the baggage that was unloaded was lost when the boat carrying it ashore swamped.

Owen Keveny had spent the summer at York Factory overseeing the dispatch of supplies to Red River and making arrangements for the Kildonan settlers' arrival. He and William Auld travelled from York Factory to meet the ship at Churchill. Auld tried to persuade the captain to fulfill his agreement to take the settlers to York Factory, but the captain claimed it was too late in the season to go any farther. The settlers were forced to spend the winter at Churchill, poorly equipped and with little food. Keveny returned home to Ireland on the ship.

One of the Kildonan women was Catherine (Kate) McPherson. In the 1920s, Kate's granddaughter recalled the stories her grandmother told about the trip. Kate began by sailing on a coastal sloop to catch the *Prince of Wales* at Stromness. The front part of the sloop's hold was formed into a huge bin that was filled with oatmeal, and the after part was occupied by a bull and cow for the settlement in Red River. The passengers had to accommodate themselves on deck.

On the *Prince of Wales*, Kate nursed the passengers who were ill with typhus, under the direction of Dr. Laserre. Following his death, the other women looked to her for leadership.

Back at the Red River, John McLean was beginning to construct Fort Douglas on the north side of Point Douglas. Miles Macdonell had left McLean in charge of the settlement while he made a fruitless trip to meet the Kildonan settlers at York Factory. Upon arriving back at The Forks in mid-October, Macdonell found that the crops had failed. The McLean family and six other men wintered at Point Douglas, but the remainder of the settlers had to return to Fort Daer (Pembina) for the winter.

# Chapter 5
# The Pemmican Proclamation

**Red River Settlement, 1814–1815**

Although the Nor'Westers made no secret of their anti-settlement feelings, open hostilities between the settlers and the Nor'Westers did not break out until the spring of 1814. Miles Macdonell was largely to blame.

An infamous document that quickly became known as the "Pemmican Proclamation," was issued on January 8, 1814, under the signatures of Miles Macdonell and Sheriff John Spencer. It began by reminding everyone that the HBC had ceded forever to the Earl of Selkirk all that tract of land known as Assiniboia and went on to state that "the welfare of the families at present forming settlements on the Red River" rendered it necessary for Macdonell "to provide for their support."

## The Pemmican Proclamation

Thus, everyone was prohibited from taking provisions out of the territory for the next 12 months unless they had a licence from Macdonell. The proclamation also stated that any provisions taken for the use of the settlement would be paid for at the customary rates. However, the final clause stated that anyone taking provisions out of the settlement without a licence would "be taken into custody and prosecuted as the laws in such cases direct." As well, any other goods that the offenders had with them when arrested would be "forfeited," along with the conveyances (boat, carts, or draft animals) used to transport the provisions.

Macdonell sent two men to personally post copies of the Pemmican Proclamation on the gates of all forts in Assiniboia. The HBC traders questioned Macdonell's authority to control the pemmican, but reluctantly allowed his men to post the orders. The Nor'Westers, on the other hand, were absolutely furious and refused to allow the proclamation to be posted at their forts.

The Nor'Westers had two strong objections. First, the proclamation put the crucial pemmican supply for the NWC fur brigades under the control of Macdonell and the HBC. Second, Macdonell was asserting that he had authority over the whole of the Red River country. The Nor'Westers argued that the territory was French Canadian by right of exploration and occupation. They also pointed to the Canada Jurisdiction Act passed by the British Parliament in 1803. That act gave the governor of Lower Canada the power to name people to act as justices for the Indian territories. These justices could hold offenders until they were conveyed to Canada for trial.

Selkirk had consulted one of the top legal experts in England about the legal status of his land grant. In the expert's opinion, the Canada Jurisdiction Act of 1803 was in conflict with the Rupert's Land Charter of 1670, which had never been repealed. The charter gave the HBC the right to administer justice in all of the country that drained into Hudson Bay. Much of the so-called Indian territories, including the Red River Settlement, drained into the Hudson Bay. Now the effect of these conflicting laws was becoming clear.

At this point, Nor'West leader William McGillivray became involved. McGillivray was the nephew of Simon McTavish, a founder of the NWC. McGillivray had arrived in Montreal in 1784, at age 20, to work for his uncle as a clerk. In 1804, following McTavish's death, McGillivray became the head of the NWC.

McGillivray's reaction to the Pemmican Proclamation was decisive. He persuaded the military authorities to reactivate a special Nor'West military unit known as the Corps of Canadian Voyageurs, which had come into existence during the War of 1812 and disbanded in the spring of 1813. McGillivray's commission as lieutenant-colonel and Archibald Norman McLeod's commission as major in the Corps were both renewed. The May 1814 order stated that commissions should be granted "to any gentlemen who should be recommended by Mr. McGillivray to serve in the

Corps of Voyageurs in the Indian and Conquered Countries."

Duncan Cameron was made a captain in the Corps, and Major McLeod, who was also justice of the peace for the Indian Territories, sent Cameron to the Red River. In addition to giving Cameron warrants to arrest those responsible for the Pemmican Proclamation, McLeod ordered Cameron to persuade the settlers to leave the settlement and go to Canada. He even lent Cameron his major's uniform to help him convince the settlers that he was an authentic military man sanctioned by the government of Canada.

In turn, Miles Macdonell seemed almost anxious to have a chance to use the five brass guns with carriages that had arrived from Scotland the previous fall. He wrote boastfully to HBC superintendent William Auld at York Factory, "I have sufficient force to crush all the North Westers in this river, should they be so hardy as to resist openly my authority." But Macdonell was forgetting two crucial factors: none of his men knew how to use these cannons, and the settlers lacked the cavalry experience that the Métis had gained as buffalo hunters.

John Wills, factor at Nor'West Fort La Souris (near Brandon House), sent a boatload of pemmican for the fur brigades down the Assiniboine River in May. Miles Macdonell swore in four special constables to keep watch on the river. Wills feared the seizure of his pemmican stock and ordered his men to hide it temporarily. Macdonell's men soon discovered the pemmican buried near White Horse Plains and took possession of 96 bags. Wills immediately met with Macdonell to protest. Macdonell offered to return part of the pemmican to Wills, but Wills refused the offer.

A few days later, Sheriff Spencer and four other men appeared at Fort La Souris. Spencer met John Pritchard, who was in charge of the fort in John Wills's absence, and demanded entry "in the King's name." Pritchard refused, saying, "You will find no entrance to this fort except a forcible one which must be at your peril." Spencer responded by breaking down the gate with two blows. Spencer and his men seized 479 bags of pemmican, 93 kegs of grease, and a large amount of meat. Spencer arrested Pritchard, but he was soon released on orders from Macdonell.

John McDonald of Garth, who was on his way to the annual Nor'West meeting at Fort William, stopped to negotiate with Macdonell. McDonald proposed that if Macdonell would let the NWC have its pemmican now, the NWC would return 175 bags for the use of the settlers over the next winter. Macdonell agreed, and an uneasy peace returned to the Red River. Sheriff Spencer resigned, angry that his actions at La Souris had been for naught. Sadly, for the sake of peace, McDonald's agreement was disavowed by the NWC partners at their annual meeting.

Pritchard's superiors labelled him a coward, saying he had not put up sufficient resistance when Spencer seized the pemmican from Fort La Souris. Pritchard responded by resigning from the NWC and travelling to Montreal for the summer. He returned to the Red River the following year and took up land as a settler.

Alexander Macdonell, Miles Macdonell's cousin, was made a Nor'West partner at the NWC annual meeting at Fort William in 1814, and he and Duncan Cameron were put in charge of the Red River Department. An important item of business at the meeting was devising a plan to destroy the Red River Settlement. Pritchard learned about this plan when he passed through Fort William on his way to Montreal.

In Pritchard's words:

> The intention of the North-West Company was to seduce and inveigle away as many of the colonists ... as they could induce to join them; and after they should thus have diminished their means of defence, to raise the Indians of Lac Rouge, Fond du Lac and other places ... to destroy the settlement ... It was also their intention to bring the Governor, Miles Macdonell, down to Montreal as a prisoner, by way of degrading the authority under which the colony was established in the eyes of the natives of that country.

In mid-July Macdonell issued another unpopular proclamation. This one prohibited the running or hunting of buffalo on horseback. As with the Pemmican Proclamation, Macdonell actually had a good reason for the buffalo measure — he was attempting to deal with the serious problem of food shortages in the settlement. Hunting on horseback scattered the buffalo over a wide area, making the buffalo hunt difficult for the settlers, who didn't have horses.

The Métis hunters naturally resented the proclamation, as they were proud of their expertise as hunters and of their skilled buffalo-hunter horses. This proclamation not only prohibited them from carrying on their traditional way of hunting but also threatened their virtual monopoly as providers of buffalo meat and pemmican.

The Nor'Westers encouraged the Métis people's resentment as part of their campaign to win them to their side against the settlers. To make matters worse for the settlers, one of the first people arrested for running buffalo was Bostonnais Pangman, whose hunting skills had kept the settlers from starving during their first winters at Pembina. Now, Pangman became an enemy of the settlement, and soon after, the NWC appointed him as one of their "Captains of the Métis."

Over the summer of 1814, the Kildonan settlers finally arrived from Churchill, one year after having left Scotland. The younger members of the group (accompanied by guides and hunters) had spent 13 days snowshoeing more than 90 kilometres south to York Factory in the early spring. They travelled single file, dragging rough sledges loaded with provisions and stores. The strongest men led the way to break trail. The women followed, and a few men brought up the rear to keep the group together and assist anyone who needed help. A Highland piper marched in the middle of the line.

They camped each day at dark, and the leader woke them by firing off his gun about 3 o'clock each morning, so they could eat breakfast and hit the trail by daybreak. Kate McPherson, the woman who had nursed the typhus sufferers, was in this party.

Although it is surprising that a woman about to give birth made the trip from Churchill on snowshoes rather than waiting to travel by boat with the older people and mothers with young children, Jean McKay apparently did just that. According to family history, on the second day of the march, Jean and her husband Angus had to stop on the trail. In a tent banked with snow, Jean gave birth to their first child, and after a short rest the young family continued the trip to York Factory alone. The rest of the group could not wait for them because of a shortage of food. After a few days' rest at York Factory, the settlers travelled the rest of the way to the Red River by boat, arriving at the settlement on June 22.

The remainder of the Kildonan group, who travelled the whole distance by water, arrived on August 25, 1814. Travelling across the Hudson Bay Lowlands from Churchill to York Factory by land is almost impossible during the short summer season, as the Lowlands are at least 80 per cent muskeg and dotted with numerous shallow lakes and meandering rivers. There is no record of the route the Kildonan settlers took. They may have travelled on the waters of Hudson

Bay itself, although the Bay is hazardous for small boats.

The settlers arrived at the Red River to find that none of the promised gardens had been planted or houses built. They had to go on to Fort Daer for the winter. Their guide for this journey was the Ojibwa (Saulteaux) Chief Peguis. He provided ponies to carry the children who were too young to walk and showed the settlers how to hunt. One of the women later told her children how the mothers bargained with Native guides to carry their children on horseback and gave small items they had brought from Scotland in payment. "More than once a poor mother, on seeing an Indian gallop away with her child, feared she would never see the child again," she told them.

The Ojibwa favoured the settlement because they saw the settlers as a new source of trade goods now that the fur trade in the Red River area was declining. They also hoped the settlers might be their military allies against the Sioux.

In July, Selkirk had written to Macdonell, reprimanding him for ignoring instructions to avoid actions that would endanger the peace. Referring to "the pemmican business," Selkirk wrote, "I am surprised that you should have thought the measures consistent with my instructions, particularly as [there was] ... a passage in my letter directly cautioning you against any act of such a tendency."

Macdonell, realizing that his position as leader of the settlement had become almost impossible, replied to Selkirk on July 24. He requested that Selkirk "not be prevented by any delicacy to send a suitable person to take my place, as I find myself unequal to the task of reconciling so many different interests."

Shortly afterwards, Macdonell travelled to York Factory, where he planned to meet the next group of settlers and escort them to the Red River. The change of scenery did not help. Macdonell apparently suffered a nervous breakdown at York Factory, such that the people around him felt it necessary to take his guns away. Macdonell confided to a doctor at York Factory that both Lord Selkirk and the settlement were ruined entirely by his mismanagement — that he was too bad to live and too great a coward to die.

While he was gone, Macdonell left Peter Fidler and Archibald McDonald, the leader of the newly arrived Kildonan settlers, in charge of the settlement. Fidler was to look after supplies and supervise the hired workmen, while McDonald was to attend to the wants of the settlers. Fidler left a detailed account in his journal of the events that occurred during that time.

On July 29, Fidler noted that the workers had completed a 15- by 23-foot kitchen (evidently in Governor Macdonell's residence) and that two women from the Highlands "hired for the purpose some time ago ... entered into their new habitation." Fidler and these cooks did not get along well. A few days later Fidler wrote, "Had another dispute with the two women in the kitchen about their using so much oatmeal. There is only Mr. McDonald and self. On Saturday night served out two pounds meal and three pints flour for us. On Monday morning the storekeeper let them have two quarts more, when I told him to give none away without an order. On Wednesday I would not allow them to have above one gallon per week which even is too much, but by the interference of Mr. McDonald, I allowed them to have that quantity. I am positive they make an improper use of some part of it."

On August 8, Fidler engaged a Canadian "to get 700 roofing sticks of 12½ by 15 feet long and to haul them to the river's edge for $10. The wood of this size is rather scarce near us." On August 17, Fidler wrote, "Indeed everyone behaves remarkably well and goes about their work with alacrity." In addition to the construction work, five men were cutting wood for charcoal, and the blacksmith was making 30 to 35 large fish hooks per day — clearly, fish was an important part of the settlers' diet, and thankfully they no longer had to fish with bent nails.

Many if not all of the settlement roofs were covered with sods. This sometimes created problems. In late September, repairs were made to the potato cellar. The roof had collapsed when its ridge pole broke. Only a few weeks later, on October 6, a house collapsed for the same reason. Fidler described the event: "Covered the house about 2/3 with sods. And as they were so heavy, and the wall plates being poplar and hewn too small, the whole roof fell in that was covered and even tore out the posts of the walls to the very foundation. Employed clearing away the wreck, and got the posts put up again, and some part of the walls. Luckily nobody received any hurt."

To gain Métis support, the Nor'Westers began to encourage the idea of the Métis as a nation — separate from both the Indians and the whites — with special rights to the land. As part of this campaign, Alexander Macdonell and Duncan Cameron appointed four Captains of the Métis — Cuthbert Grant Jr., William Shaw, Bostonnais Pangman, and Nicholas (Bonhomme) Montour.

One of the Métis captains, Cuthbert Grant, was born at Fort de la Rivière Tremblante (near present-day Kamsack, Saskatchewan) in 1793. His father was a longtime Nor'West employee who became a wintering partner in 1795, and his mother was Cree-Métis. Grant's father died when he was six, and Nor'West leader William McGillivray became his guardian. McGillivray took him to Montreal to be educated. Grant may also have spent some time in Scotland, but the records are unclear. At any rate, he was quite well educated. He began working in the NWC's Montreal office around 1810, and in 1812 he was appointed as a clerk at Fort Espérance on the Qu'Appelle River under John Pritchard. Two of Cuthbert's sisters, Mary and Josephete, married Métis poet and songwriter Pierre Falcon and Nor'West factor John Wills respectively.

Duncan Cameron preferred to offer incentives to persuade the settlers to leave but was willing to use violence if necessary. His door was always open to the settlers, along with a blazing fire, good food, and drink. He could talk to them in Gaelic and gave them supplies when they were short.

The settlers saw him as a government official and trusted what he said because he wore a military uniform and signed himself as "Captain, Voyageur Corps, Commanding Officer, Red River." Over the winter of 1814–1815, Cameron warned the settlers that Native peoples might attack in the spring. He claimed that the settlers' only hope for survival was to accept the NWC offer of free transportation to Canada, free provisions, 200 acres of land, and other inducements. By spring he had convinced about three-quarters of the settlers to accept land near Owen Sound in Upper Canada.

In April 1815, Cameron prevailed upon a group of settlers to take possession of the settlement's arms and transport them from Fort Douglas to Fort Gibraltar. The settlers evidently agreed to do so after Cameron circulated a rumour that the HBC would use the guns to prevent the settlers from leaving. When the settlement's officers arrested one of their own men for assisting in this operation, a party that included Grant broke into the governor's house and released the prisoner.

In late May, Alexander Macdonell arrived at the Red River from Qu'Appelle with 12 Cree to launch a war of nerves against the settlement. The visitors wore war paint and charged through the community at night, shooting. Twelve of the settlement's horses were later found shot dead by arrows. This series of hit-and-run raids against the settlement became known as the "Pemmican War."

To cover the departure of the NWC canoes carrying 42 colonists east to Canada, Grant set up camp on the Red River in early June. His camp was downstream from Fort Douglas at Frog Plain (Seven Oaks). Grant's men also harried the settlement, and the settlers and the Métis exchanged gunfire on several occasions.

Finally, on June 16, 1815, Macdonell surrendered to the Nor'Westers in hopes that his departure would save the settlement. He left Peter Fidler in charge. Chief Peguis unsuccessfully tried to intervene on behalf of the settlers.

On June 25, Fidler was forced to sign a treaty that was also signed by "the four chiefs of the half-breeds" (the Captains of the Métis) on behalf of the Nor'Westers and the Métis. The first term of the treaty read, "All settlers to retire immediately from this river, and no appearance of a colony to remain."

The second and third terms of the treaty were more conciliatory. The second stated, "Peace and amity to subsist between all parties ... in future, throughout these two rivers, and on no account any person to be molested in his lawful pursuits." The third said, "Every person retiring peaceable from this river immediately, shall not be molested in their passage out."

The Nor'Westers and Métis burned down all the settlement buildings except one, including the four houses forming the fort, outbuildings, the mill, and about 20 settlers' houses. Only the blacksmith shop, which was held by four men who had barricaded themselves inside, was left standing.

After Fidler surrendered, Grant returned to his post on

the Qu'Appelle River. The settlement families who hadn't already gone with the Nor'Westers left for Jack River at the north end of Lake Winnipeg, escorted by members of Peguis's band. Reports were that Peguis had wept over the ashes of Governor Macdonell's house.

Only the men who had held the blacksmith shop remained at the ruined settlement. Their leader, John McLeod, later described what happened after the settlers left. The men had carried a small cannon (a three- or four-pounder) to the blacksmith shop, along with all the cart chains they could find and some powder. They chopped up the chain for shot and fired at their attackers, saving the post "from utter destruction and pillage."

The only human casualty of the Pemmican War was an HBC employee named John Warren, who was accidentally killed early in the conflict when an HBC gun exploded. Although McLeod and his men were unable to save the settlement, they succeeded in keeping "from 800 to 1000 pounds worth of attractive trade goods belonging to the HBC untouched."

## Chapter 6
# Howling among Wolves

**The Forks, 1815–1816**

Colin Robertson, formerly an employee of the NWC, was almost single-handedly responsible for returning the settlers to their ruined settlement. Robertson was tall, with wild curly red hair, long sideburns, and a hooked nose. He was a romantic who was fond of Shakespeare, Madeira wine, and fine china, but also a man of action, and — despite his arrogance and flamboyance — a capable leader. He summed up his philosophy in these few words: "Glittering pomposity has an amazing effect on the freemen, Métis, and Indians. When you are among wolves, howl."

Robertson had resigned from the NWC in 1809 because he felt he was not promoted quickly enough. He had also clashed with Nor'West colleague John McDonald of Garth, with whom he once fought a duel. After leaving the NWC, Robertson tried to convince the HBC to expand their trade into the Athabasca country northwest of Rupert's Land, and finally the HBC agreed to let him mount an Athabasca expedition. In May 1815, he left Lower Canada in command of a brigade of 16 canoes and 160 voyageurs.

In early July, Robertson's brigade met a guide who told them that the Red River Settlement had been destroyed and Miles Macdonell arrested. Macdonell's son, who was travelling in Robertson's brigade, did not seem surprised. He commented to Robertson, "It's too true Mr. R. My father has and always will be unfortunate."

A few days later, Robertson met the Nor'West brigade that was transporting Macdonell to Lower Canada as a prisoner. Macdonell was accompanied by about a dozen Nor'West partners as a guard, for they were determined not to let him escape. However, he was allowed to speak briefly to his son, as well as to Robertson about the settlement's affairs.

As a result of this meeting, Robertson decided to send the main body of his brigade on ahead, while he made a side trip to the Red River. On July 14, Robertson met Chief Peguis, who was encamped with a large group of his followers. Peguis made a long speech. Robertson said that Peguis "found much fault with the NWC and seemed anxious" for Robertson to attempt to re-establish the settlement.

Robertson then visited the ruins of the settlement, where John McLeod and his colleagues remained in charge. "Mr.

McLeod appears to be an active intelligent young man and deserves much credit for remaining here," Robertson wrote.

By late July, Robertson had reached the settlers at Jack River and tried to convince them to return to Point Douglas. On August 5, he told them he planned to leave for the Red River on August 8 with everyone who wished to accompany him. He also made it clear that he would not permit any contact between the settlers and the Nor'Westers. A group of 35 settlers in three boats returned to The Forks. Since 60 people had apparently fled north from the settlement, 25 either returned to Scotland or remained in the north.

When Robertson and the settlers reached The Forks on August 19, they discovered that things were not as bad as expected. As soon as the Nor'Westers had gone, McLeod and his colleagues had set to work to restore the settlement. When the settlement was burned, the attackers had trampled the fields in an attempt to destroy the crops. Even so, McLeod's crew was able to harvest 400 bushels of wheat, 200 bushels of barley, 500 bushels of potatoes, and some peas and oats. The men also made hay, built fences, and began constructing new buildings and repairing damaged ones.

Robertson decided to build a new fort on Point Douglas "as it is well situated for a place of defence and has a beautiful prospect of the plains and commands two angles of the river." Robertson sent five Canadian servants to cut down pickets and square logs to begin putting Point Douglas in some state of defence before the Nor'Westers returned.

On September 3, Robertson hired Jean-Baptiste Lagimodière to cart home the grain and hay with his horses, as the only two workhorses left to the settlement were carrying provisions from Fort Daer. Robertson wrote, "This is really a hard circumstance considering the number of horses that belonged to the colony last year. His Lordship will require to estimate his damages pretty high for his losses have been great."

In mid-October, Chief Peguis arrived for another visit, bringing with him 65 of his tribesmen and their families. He announced his arrival by sending gifts of wild rice, dried meat, and sturgeon on ahead. In turn, Robertson prepared for the visitors by laying aside gifts of ammunition (gun powder, balls, and flints), tobacco, blankets, liquor, and cloth.

When Peguis was approaching Fort Douglas, his men fired a volley. The settlers returned the salute with a three-pounder gun and hoisted their flag. Peguis immediately responded by mounting his colours at the end of his canoe. Robertson described the scene: "... and then the whole squadron came in sight consisting of nearly 150 canoes ... It had a wild but grand appearance — their bodies painted in various colours — their heads decorated, some with branches and others with feathers. Every time we fired the cannon the woods re-echoed with that wild whoop of joy, which they gave to denote the satisfaction they received."

The women and children paddled past the fort and set up their camp on the spot designated by Robertson, while the men were invited into the largest room in the fort, which they entered "with three hearty cheers from our people." After everyone was seated, Robertson ordered the lighting of a large peace calumet (pipe). Robertson took two or three puffs and then presented it to Peguis. Robertson wrote that Peguis "... after smoking about a minute passed it to the next in respectability to himself, and in this manner it went round the band. During this ceremony not a single word or even a whisper was heard." Then Robertson had his interpreter deliver his speech to the assembly.

A few days later, Robertson received word that Alexander Macdonell had attacked the HBC post at Qu'Appelle. Robertson decided he had to strike a blow at Fort Gibraltar, even though he had only 20 men. Almost immediately after making this decision, Robertson learned that Nor'Westers Duncan Cameron and Seraphim Lamar were being brought to Fort Douglas from Fort Gibraltar as prisoners. Robertson told Cameron that he must deliver up all the arms the Nor'Westers had taken to Fort Gibraltar the previous April. Cameron had no choice but to agree and sent Lamar to let Robertson's men into Gibraltar. As soon as Peguis and his men learned what was going on, they came to the settlers' assistance.

Justifying his actions in his journal, Robertson wrote that he had ordered his men to treat the prisoners well and respect their private property. Although he planned to release Cameron almost immediately, Robertson believed that having captured and held him even briefly served "to lower his consequence a little," which was necessary for the safety of the settlement. "I will remove all the arms in his Fort to this place until tranquility is established in that quarter. These are points I will insist upon."

The next day Robertson had a boat move all the arms and ammunition from Fort Gibraltar to Fort Douglas. Then he addressed the prisoners:

> Gentlemen, the cruelty with which you exercised the power ... placed in your hands last spring deserves a greater punishment than I am willing to inflict ... But to see what effect a generous action will have on you, you shall be released and put in possession of your fort on the following mild conditions: First that an express be sent to Qu'Appelle to put a stop to the violent measure of your Mr. Macdonell, and that you will not either directly or indirectly attempt to seduce any emigrants that the Earl of Selkirk has, or will in future send to this country.

Cameron agreed and was released.

Then Robertson learned that Robert Semple had been named Governor-in-Chief of the HBC territories with a controlling power over the settlement. Semple would be arriving within two weeks with 80 new colonists.

Robertson was not pleased. "It is astonishing that no

Robert Semple

instructions have been sent me ... Do they mean to take us by surprise with such a number of families?" He knew Selkirk was on his way to Montreal, so he hired Jean-Baptiste Lagimodière to carry a message to Selkirk.

Both Miles Macdonell and Colin Robertson held Lagimodière in high regard. Unlike most of the buffalo hunters and former voyageurs, Lagimodière tried to remain neutral.

He hoped that the Red River Settlement would succeed so that he could make a permanent home there for his wife, Marie-Anne, and their children. Marie-Anne would have preferred to return to her home in Quebec, but Jean-Baptiste loved the West and had no intention of leaving it. Living in a settlement at the Red River seemed an ideal compromise.

Robertson agreed that Marie-Anne and her four young children could live at Fort Douglas during Jean-Baptiste's absence; and that, in the event of his death, the HBC would pay her an annuity of seven pounds for the next 10 years.

Selkirk was well aware of the problems facing his settlement. After unsuccessfully requesting military protection from the British Colonial Office, Selkirk decided to go to Montreal in September 1815, to challenge the NWC on its own ground. Government officials in Lower Canada were no more willing than the Colonial Office had been to provide the military force Selkirk felt was needed — even though Selkirk had guaranteed to underwrite the cost involved if the military expedition later proved to have been unnecessary. The officials did give Selkirk (along with Robert Semple and two other men) the legal authority to act as a magistrate and justice of the peace in "Indian Country." Selkirk spent the winter in Montreal making preparations to go to the Red River in the spring.

Selkirk had naturally not been happy about the resurrected Corps of Canadian Voyageurs, which lent legitimacy to Duncan Cameron and materially assisted him in persuading so many of the settlers to abandon the Red River in the spring of 1815. Selkirk was now successful in persuading Sir John Sherbrooke, Governor of Lower Canada, to "cancel and annul" the commissions that McGillivray had arranged for in 1814.

Part of Selkirk's preparations included recruiting 90 soldiers from two Swiss mercenary regiments (de Meuron and de Watteville) that had come to Canada to fight in the War of 1812. Following the war, these regiments had been disbanded, and the soldiers were being demobilized when Selkirk arrived. He offered them free land if they would travel to the Red River to restore the settlement and then remain as settlers after peace was established. These soldier-settlers became known as the de Meurons.

Back at the Red River, Robertson officially welcomed Governor Semple on November 3, 1815. The settlers (120 colonists and servants in total) arrived the next day. Many of them were in large family groups. According to the ship's passenger list, 63 of the settlers shared only five surnames. They included 18 McKays, 12 Mathesons, 12 Sutherlands, 11 Bannermans, and 10 McBeths. A check of the 2004 Winnipeg telephone directory shows that many families with these names continue to live at the Red River. All of these names are also commemorated in Winnipeg's street names.

When Semple expressed his regret that Robertson had returned Fort Gibraltar to the Nor'Westers, Robertson replied, "I will give you Cameron and the fort whenever you choose."

Semple and Robertson disliked each other from the beginning. Robertson judged Semple "a proud Englishman, rather too conscious of his own abilities." At first Semple respected Robertson's superior knowledge of the country, but eventually he asserted his leadership. Semple was a brave man, but he lacked the experience needed to deal with the situation he found himself in. He listened to conflicting advice and thus appeared weak and vacillating. For example, he alternated between taking aggressive steps against the Métis and attempting to reconcile with them.

Robertson, perhaps unfairly, accused Semple of having contempt for the Métis. Robertson realized the settlement would never succeed unless he loosened the ties between the Métis and the Nor'Westers. He paid top prices for everything he bought from the Métis and gave them presents from the HBC's trade goods. He had also managed to reconcile with Bostonnais Pangman, who was again hunting for the settlers at Fort Daer.

Once again, most of the settlers had to spend the winter at Fort Daer, and Robertson worried about the food situation. On November 6 he wrote, "The settlers employed this day in thrashing out wheat and barley for their passage to Fort Daer, as they have ate up the little dried provisions I had here. It was very cold last night. I'm afraid they will be taken by the ice. These people will be hard upon the grain and I am anxious to preserve a sufficient quantity for seed."

In early winter, Semple left for a tour of inspection to Brandon House and Qu'Appelle. The winter of 1815–1816 passed in an uneasy quiet, with the settlers relatively well fed.

Construction work continued at the Red River throughout the winter, but Robertson found his Scottish countrymen lacking as carpenters: "I would do twice the quantity of work with Canadians and still more if I had Americans. A Scotch carpenter works in this country as if he was paying 2 shillings per foot for his wood."

Cuthbert Grant had emerged as a leader on the Nor'West side, and Duncan Cameron named him "Captain-General of all the Half-Breeds" in March 1816. On March 13, Grant wrote to Cameron from Qu'Appelle:

> I believe it is more than Colin Robertson ... dare to offer the least insult to any of the Bois-Brûlés [Métis] ... He shall see that it is neither fifteen, thirty, nor fifty of his best horsemen that can make [us] ... bow to him ... It is hoped we shall come off with flying colours, and never to see any of them again in the colonizing way in Red River...We are all to remain at the Forks [this] ... summer, for fear they should play us the same trick as last summer, of coming back; but they shall receive a warm reception [if they do] ...

By the time Cameron returned to Fort Gibraltar from Qu'Appelle in early March, Robertson had come to mistrust his intentions towards the settlers. As a test, Robertson sent his servant "over to Cameron to play the discontented."

Robertson's suspicions were confirmed. Cameron offered the servant free passage to Montreal.

About the same time Alexander Macdonell wrote, "I remark with pleasure the hostile proceedings of our neighbours [the Métis] ... A storm is gathering ... ready to burst on the rascals who deserve it ... The new nation under their leaders are coming forward to clear their native soil of intruders and assassins."

On March 19, Robertson intercepted another letter from Alexander Macdonell to Cameron that hinted strongly of an attack on the settlement. "You will see some sport at Red River before the month of June is over ... Never was our danger so great ... William Shaw is collecting all the Half-Breeds ... and has ordered his friends to prepare for the field ..."

Robertson decided to retake Fort Gibraltar without waiting for Semple to return and give his permission. With a force of 17, Robertson seized the fort for the second time in six months. He pillaged all property in the fort, including 50 packs of furs. Nor'Wester Jean-Baptiste Branconnier, who was captured in the fort, later testified, "I was wounded by one of the party who took the fort, but I am not sure by whom. The conduct of this party who took possession of the fort ... was violent and outrageous ... so much so that I was afraid we would all be murdered by them. They put pistols to our heads and threatened to blow our brains out."

When Governor Semple returned from Brandon House, he approved of Robertson's actions. Semple charged Cameron with multiple offences: seducing settlers to desert Selkirk and servants to desert and defraud their masters, encouraging Métis to destroy the settlement, wounding and causing the death of people defending their property, destroying "English cattle brought here at an immense expense," carrying off large amounts of property, and "encouraging Indians tribes to make war upon British subjects."

After reading these charges to Cameron, Semple shipped him to York Factory along with Branconnier and two other servants. From there, they were to be sent to stand trial in England.

In the meantime, Lagimodière had spent the winter travelling across the country, mainly on snowshoes. In early March he arrived in Montreal and delivered Robertson's letter to Selkirk. Selkirk sent Lagimodière back with a reply to Semple. The message stated that it would be "necessary to use force" to compel the NWC to leave the area of the Red River Settlement, and that Selkirk was "anxious that this should be done under legal warrant."

On his return trip, Lagimodière was waylaid by Nor'West agents at Fond du Lac (near Duluth, Minnesota). He was beaten, robbed, and taken to Fort William as a prisoner, and Selkirk's letter to Semple fell into Nor'West hands.

Selkirk headed for Fort William in mid-June 1816, accompanied by his 90 de Meuron recruits and a six-man bodyguard of regular soldiers. His friends had prevailed upon Governor Sherbrooke to send the bodyguard due to fears that the Nor'Westers might attack Selkirk.

Earlier on, Semple had sent HBC clerk Pierre-Chrysologue Pambrun to get supplies for the settlers from the HBC's house at Fort Qu'Appelle. Pambrun began his return trip on May 1, leaving Qu'Appelle with 22 men in five canoes. They were carrying 600 bags of pemmican and 22 bales of fur. For the next few days Métis scouts watched the progress of Pambrun's brigade from the hills overlooking the Qu'Appelle River. At the same time, the main force under Cuthbert Grant moved quietly over the upper plains, out of sight until the brigade neared a point on the river called Grand Rapids. Here, Grant led his men down a ravine to the valley bottom and captured the boats as they passed through the rapids in single file.

Pambrun, a veteran of the Corps of Canadian Voyageurs, gave a detailed account of his experiences.

> As we were going down the river on the 5th of May ... a party of armed Bois-Brûlés ... surrounded me, and forced me to give up the boats and furs, and the pemmican ... Cuthbert Grant, Peter Pangman, and Thomas McKay were of the party who made me a prisoner. I was taken back to River Qu'Appelle ... [and] kept there for five days. Mr. Alexander Macdonell was in command, and I asked him ... by whose orders I had been arrested? He said it was by his own ...

Pambrun also recorded a speech given by Alexander Macdonell to some local Natives (likely Cree), as well as the chief's response to Macdonell's words::

> I address you bashfully, for I have not a pipe of tobacco to give you. All our goods have been taken by the English, but we are now upon a party to drive them away. Those people have been spoil- ing the fair lands which belong to you and the Bois-Brûlés, and to which they have no right. They have been driving away the buffalo. You will soon be poor and miserable if the English stay; but we will drive them away if the Indians do not, for the NWC and the Bois-Brûlés are one ...

> The chief said that he knew nothing about it, and should not go himself; if some of the young men went, it was nothing to him...[Macdonell replied,] 'We are determined to drive them away, and if they make any resistance, your land shall be drenched with their blood.'...

Pambrun soon learned that the Nor'Westers had also attacked Brandon House. Peter Fidler, master of Brandon House, said that about 50 Métis, Indians, and freemen, arrived on horseback. They were flying the Métis flag, beating drums, and singing native songs. Grant demanded that Fidler deliver to him the keys of the stores and warehouses. When Fidler refused, Grant's men broke open the buildings and plundered them of every article they contained, except for the packs of furs. They also stole private property from everyone in Brandon House and all of the horses belonging to the HBC and the non-Métis employees. Pangman told Fidler that they had plundered the house because Colin Robertson had taken their fort at The Forks.

Robertson wanted the pemmican that Grant had captured from Pambrun and Fidler to be recaptured by force, but Semple decided to wait for Grant's party to come to the settlement. Semple also rejected Robertson's suggestion that the settlers stay near Fort Douglas for safety, rather than dispersing to their individual lots. Semple accepted only one of Robertson's suggestions — that the settlers dismantle Fort Gibraltar and use the logs to strengthen Fort Douglas.

Robertson, feeling that his situation had become impossible, decided to leave the Red River on June 11. Some of the settlers wanted to go with him, but Semple convinced them to stay. According to Robertson, Semple also said, "Don't leave me, Mr. Robertson. I entreat you on Lord Selkirk's account not to leave the settlement at this juncture."

The next day Robertson reconsidered his decision to leave. He wrote in his journal that he left his camp early in the morning with his spirits much depressed. He described his thoughts as follows:

Shall I return and be obliged to bear fresh indignities from these inexperienced men? Will Governor Semple follow my advice, or will he be governed by the bravados of his officers? Will my presence unite or disunite — this is the point. Were they unanimous and prudent they have nothing to fear ... but the contempt with which they treat the enemy is what alarms me the most.

Finally, Robertson decided to turn back to Fort Douglas. He sent a note on ahead to Semple offering to return, but Semple refused the offer. Robertson was "grieved and disappointed" at the reply. "How could I ever dream of such an answer after what passed between us the day we parted? This adds one more to the many proofs that this gentleman is governed by the opinion of others."

In the meantime, Pambrun, still a prisoner of the Nor'Westers, had reached Portage la Prairie. On the morning of June 17, the Bois-Brûlés set off from Portage la Prairie on horseback. They were well-armed with guns, pistols, lances, and bows and arrows. Alexander Macdonell and 30 or 40 men remained behind. Pambrun later described what he believed were the Nor'Westers' plans that day. He said their object was to take Fort Douglas and break up the settlement. The settlers were to be starved out of the fort. "If any of them went out to fish or get water, they were to be shot if they could not be taken prisoners."

## Chapter 7
# The Battle of Seven Oaks

**Red River Settlement, June 1816**

The Nor'Westers said that when they left Portage la Prairie their plans were only to take the pemmican captured from Qu'Appelle and Brandon House to the fur brigade from the east. They would meet at Post Bas-de-la-Rivière, where the Winnipeg River flows into Lake Winnipeg, and the fur brigade would then distribute the pemmican to posts farther north and west.

Although Pambrun believed the Nor'Westers intended to take Fort Douglas, Grant's actions do not support that view. Alexander Macdonell later said he had ordered Grant to travel by canoe as far as The Passage (a point on the Assiniboine River just inside the present-day western boundary of Winnipeg).

There, Grant was to transfer the pemmican to Red River carts and proceed northeast across country to La Grenouillère (Frog Plain) or Seven Oaks, avoiding, if possible, being discovered by the Hudson's Bay people and settlers.

Macdonell stated that "upon no account [was Grant's force] to molest any of the settlers." The Nor'Westers definitely wished to destroy the settlement, but it appears that in this instance their chief concern was to get the pemmican supplies safely to Bas-de-la-Rivière.

The plan was for Grant's party to meet some Canadian freemen at Frog Plain, who would inform him whether the Nor'West brigade had arrived at Lake Winnipeg to pick up the pemmican. If the canoes had not yet arrived, Grant and his party were to camp at least nine kilometres below the settlement and await their arrival. Macdonell wanted scouts to send him "immediate notice" when the canoes arrived.

Grant was unable to leave the river at The Passage as planned. Much of the land near the Assiniboine River was low and marshy, and a wet spring had made it impassable for the carts. Consequently, Grant had to travel at least another eight kilometres to Catfish (Omand's) Creek. Leaving the river at Catfish Creek brought Grant's party much closer to The Forks than originally intended. Even here, the land was swampy, and the horses were sometimes up to their bellies in water and mud.

Chief Peguis, having advance word that the Métis were coming, offered the services of about 70 of his men to help protect the settlers. Semple declined, but Marie-Anne Lagimodière accepted Peguis's invitation to move with her children from Fort Douglas to Peguis's camp.

John Pritchard, who had resigned from the NWC two years earlier and returned to the Red River as a settler, wrote a detailed description of what happened at Seven Oaks. His account is now considered the most accurate and unbiased description of this controversial affair.

The first intimation of trouble came early on the afternoon of June 19. The lookout in the watchtower at Fort Douglas gave the alarm as soon as he caught the first indistinct sight of a party of horsemen riding across the plains. Governor Semple hurried into the tower and watched the riders through a spyglass for some minutes. Certain they were Métis, he called for 15 or 20 volunteers to go out and meet them. He waited impatiently while the men were issued weapons — muskets, bayonets, balls, and powder — but refused to take the three-pounder field piece (cannon), saying he was only going to see what the Métis wanted, not fight with them.

As Semple and his men marched down the trail leading from the fort to the settlement, they met several settlers heading for the safety of the fort. The settlers told Semple that the Métis force was quite large. They suggested that he would need two field pieces in order to face them. Semple sent storekeeper John Bourke back for one cannon, but resumed the march without waiting for it.

In the meantime, the Métis, led by Cuthbert Grant, came across three settlers working in a field and took them prisoner so they could not raise the alarm. Then, seeing Semple and his men marching towards them, Grant ordered a small advance party to make camp while he and the main party rode back to meet Semple.

The two forces met at Seven Oaks. They halted when they came within hailing distance of each other. The two groups faced each other silently and motionlessly — Grant's men on horseback, Semple's on foot. Grant had roughly twice as many men as Semple. Most were Métis, but there were also a few Canadians and Natives. Semple's force was composed mainly of HBC servants, with only a few settlers.

Pritchard, who accompanied Semple that day, wrote that the Métis, "with their faces painted in the most hideous manner and in the dress of Indians warriors, came forward and surrounded us in the form of a half moon." Semple's men extended their line and moved onto the open plain. Then, as Grant's men advanced, Semple's retreated a few steps.

Grant gave an order to one of his men, a Canadian named François Fermin Boucher: "Tell Semple to surrender, or we will fire upon him." Boucher rode up to Semple, waving his hand and calling out, "What do you want?"

Semple replied, "What do you want yourself?"

"We want our fort," Boucher said, referring to Robertson's seizure of Fort Gibraltar in the spring.

Semple responded, "Go to your fort."

By this time Boucher and Semple were almost touching and were no longer speaking loudly enough for Pritchard to hear, but other reports quote Boucher as replying, "Miserable rogue, why have you destroyed our fort?"

Then Semple lost his temper. He shouted, "Wretch, do you dare to speak so to me?" He seized the reins of Boucher's horse and may have grabbed at his gun. A second later a shot rang out.

According to Pritchard's account, "Almost immediately a general discharge of firearms took place, but whether it began on our side or that of the enemy, it was impossible to distinguish. My attention was then directed to my personal defence." Pritchard described how one man was shot while trying to give himself up. He raised his hands and in English and broken French called in vain for mercy. One man shot him through the head and another "cut open his belly with a knife." Fortunately for Pritchard, one of the Canadians saved him "from sharing the fate of my friend ... After this I was reserved from death in the most providential manner no less than six different times ... With the exception of myself, no quarter was given to any of us."

Grant wounded Semple with a shot that shattered his hip. Semple said, "I am not mortally wounded and if you could get me conveyed to the fort, I think I should live." Grant promised this would be done and left Semple in the care of a Canadian. The Canadian, who either would not or could not carry out Grant's instructions, later said that "an Indian of their party had shot Mr. Semple in the breast."

While Semple's men were armed, most of their guns were in such a state of disrepair as to be almost useless. Grant's men, who naturally did not know this, believed the governor's party was a threat to them. Red River fur trader and historian J. J. Hargrave wrote some 50 years later, "The infatuation which led the Governor's party to attempt, by a vain exhibition of useless weapons, to intimidate nearly three times their number of men to whom the saddle and the gun were instruments of their daily occupation is almost incomprehensible."

Boucher, the man who came forward to speak to Semple at the beginning of the battle, was later taken as a prisoner to Montreal. There, he declared before a justice of the peace that he did not kill anyone and that Alexander Macdonell had only sent him to carry provisions from Portage la Prairie to Frog Plain. He said they passed at a distance from Fort Douglas to avoid being seen by the settlers, although he admitted that they carried off one of the settlers "with a view of weakening the Hudson's Bay party."

When Grant's force saw Semple and his men advancing with muskets in their hands, Boucher said, they feared the HBC men meant to harm them. The Métis wanted to fire on Semple immediately, but Boucher said he objected and advanced alone to speak to Semple. Semple then took hold of the butt end of Boucher's gun and ordered his men to advance. The men did not obey. Boucher told them that if they fired, they were all dead men. Semple told his men not to be afraid and ordered them to fire.

Immediately after that, Boucher heard two musket shots fired by the HBC men. He threw himself from his horse, though still holding on to its mane, and the horse dragged him about the distance of a gun shot away. He remained there throughout the rest of the battle.

According to Boucher, about 64 Nor'Westers were assembled "for the purpose of taking the Hudson's Bay fort by famine," but only about 30 were involved at the beginning of the battle.

After the initial shots were fired, the Métis took cover behind their horses and fired a volley of shots. When they threw themselves to the ground to reload, Semple's men, thinking the Métis had been hit, cheered too soon.

By the time the battle was over, Semple and 20 of his men had been killed. The dead included one settler, 15 HBC servants, Semple's secretary, the surgeon, and two military men. Of all the men who had started out from Fort Douglas that afternoon, only seven survived.

Many of the settlers thought the first shot at Seven Oaks was fired by a Lieutenant Holt when his gun went off accidentally. There was no proof of this, one way or the other, since Holt was killed. The whole battle took only about 15 minutes. The men who survived escaped into the woods and made their way back to Fort Douglas, where all was in confusion as the settlers crowded into the fort for protection.

Peguis and his men went out the following day to collect the bodies and carry them to the fort in carts. According to tradition, some bodies were not recovered, having been dragged away by wild animals.

Grant took John Pritchard prisoner after the battle. Six settlers, including one woman and two children, had also been taken prisoner before the battle began. Grant told Pritchard he had not expected to fight that day. He thought the conflict would take the form of scattered ambushes and an attempt to starve the settlers into abandoning the settlement.

Having negotiated terms of surrender with Grant, Pritchard was allowed to deliver the terms to the fort. Grant then reverted from military leader to Nor'West clerk. He took inventory of all the goods and equipment in the fort and prepared a declaration that he signed, as did the settlers and HBC people.

The declaration stated that all hostilities were to cease and all prisoners immediately released. If the settlers and HBC traders gave up all public property, the Métis would give them safe escort and allow them to take their personal effects with them. The group was to be allowed sufficient provisions and boats to travel to York Factory.

The settlers and HBC men left for Jack River at the north end of Lake Winnipeg, as they had done the previous year after Miles Macdonell's arrest. However, within a few days a party of senior Nor'West officials intercepted them. In spite of the agreement made with Grant, they arrested Pritchard and several other men and took them to Fort William.

Pritchard was not actually in charge of the settlement after Governor Semple's death. Confusingly, that honour fell to a man named Alexander Macdonell — not Nor'Wester Alexander Macdonell who had been trying to destroy the settlement, but another man of the same name. This second Alexander Macdonell had been named councillor and sheriff of Assiniboia in January and became second-in-command to Semple when Robertson left the settlement.

Charles Bottineau, a freeman who arrived at the Red River some 10 or 12 days after the battle, spoke with four men who had been involved in the battle — La Serpe, Antoine Hoole, and François Deschamps (father and son). La Serpe boasted of having killed two Englishmen with his own hands and showed Bottineau clothes he claimed to have removed from their dead bodies. La Serpe said he was determined to prevent the English from setting foot in the country again. He said that if free Canadians like Bottineau did not help to plunder and drive out the English, they themselves would be driven out. Nor'West partner Alexander Macdonell, who was present at the time, heaped praise on La Serpe.

The Métis poet and songwriter Pierre Falcon commemorated the events of Seven Oaks in a song. Falcon and Grant were close friends and brothers-in-law.

Like most of the Métis, Falcon could not write, so his poems and songs were not written down until late in his life.

Therefore, it is not known whether the following version (one of many) is close to the original, or how well it has been translated from French to English.

### *Chanson de la Grenouillère*

*Would you like to hear me sing of a true and*
*recent thing?*
*It was June 19th, the band of Bois-Brûlés arrived*
*that day.*
*Oh the brave warriors they!*

*Now we like honourable men did act.*
*Sent an ambassador —*
*Yes, in fact, Monsieur Governor, would you*
*like to stay?*
*A moment spare — There's something we'd*
*like to say."*

*Governor, Governor, full of ire.*
*"Soldiers!" he cries, "Fire! Fire!'*
*So they fire the first and their muskets roar!*
*They almost kill our ambassador.*

*You should have seen those Englishmen —*
*Bois-Brûlés chasing them, chasing them.*

*The Battle of Seven Oaks*

*From bluff to bluff they stumbled that day*
*While the Bois-Brûlés shouted, "Hurray!"*

*Tell oh tell me who made up this song?*
*Why it's our own poet, Pierre Falcon.*

# Chapter 8
# "The Trading Lord" Takes Fort William

**Fort William, 1816–1817**

Selkirk did not learn of the disaster at Seven Oaks until he reached Sault Ste. Marie on July 25. He immediately left for Fort William. When his flotilla arrived there on August 12 — to the sound of drums, pipes, and trumpets — his first action was to demand the release of everyone the Nor'Westers had imprisoned. This included John Pritchard and five other men who had been at Seven Oaks, as well as Jean-Baptiste Lagimodière and the men who were with him when he was waylaid while carrying Selkirk's message to the Red River.

After interviewing the prisoners, Selkirk concluded that all the Nor'West partners were implicated in the battle of Seven Oaks. In his capacity as magistrate, he ordered the arrest of Nor'West leader William McGillivray on charges of "conspiracy, treason and being accessory to murder." Immediately afterwards the de Meurons arrested all the other partners in the fort. One of the de Meuron officers later described the arrest:

> [Because the soldiers] were dressed half in uniform and half in civilian clothes, and we the officers ... were armed with swords and pistols, we resembled a band of robbers ... Our men ... were in no mood to fool around, and broke down the gate. Fortunately no shot was fired, otherwise we could not have restrained our men from plundering, and in all likelihood blood would have been spilled.

A search of the fort found a large number of guns hidden in a hayloft, along with eight barrels of gunpowder. The fort blacksmith reported that the weapons had been concealed "to affect the rescue of the partners arrested and to destroy the party of the Earl of Selkirk." Fearing a massacre, Selkirk seized Fort William.

McGillivray accepted no personal or company responsibility for the events at Seven Oaks. He argued that Cuthbert Grant "considers his situation as [Métis] chief more important than his office as [Nor'West] clerk," and therefore it would have been dangerous for the Nor'Westers to interfere. He also said the Métis were justified in arming themselves because Semple had gone out to attack them.

Selkirk arrested nine men in total and sent them to Canada for trial on August 17. Nine days later, a severe gale caused one of the three canoes carrying the prisoners to capsize on Lake Superior, and nine men were drowned. The dead included one Nor'West partner, two de Meurons, and six Iroquois paddlers hired to take the prisoners and their guards to Montreal. McGillivray later complained that the canoes were overloaded, charging that one canoe suitable for 15 passengers carried 22.

When McGillivray arrived in Montreal following his arrest by Selkirk, he demanded to be released on bail. He also asked Sir John Sherbrooke, Governor of Lower Canada, to order that Fort William be handed back to the Nor'Westers and Selkirk be arrested.

Selkirk's wife had already written to Governor Sherbrooke in August, suggesting that Sherbrooke appoint two people "invested with the authority of government to enquire into the nature and causes of these atrocities." Not surprisingly, given McGillivray's high position, he was released on bail almost immediately, and a warrant was sent out for Selkirk's arrest.

The British government, alarmed at the events at the Red River and Fort William, also sent a sternly worded letter to Sherbrooke. The letter ordered the governor to require the return of all buildings and property seized during the dispute to whoever was in possession of them before the conflict broke out. It also ordered the removal of any blockades to allow "all persons to pursue their usual and accustomed trade without hindrance or molestation."

In the fall of 1816, Lower Canada appointed a two-man commission of inquiry headed by William B. Coltman, an English-born Quebec businessman. Coltman and his fellow commissioner, John Fletcher, spent the winter beginning their investigations in Montreal.

A retired Nor'West partner, Daniel McKenzie, remained at Fort William after the nine active partners were arrested and sent to Montreal. Several months earlier, McGillivray, learning that Selkirk was on his way to Fort William, had engaged McKenzie to buy up all the supplies at the Michilimackinac and Drummond Island posts and deliver them to Fort William. Presumably this was an attempt to run the Selkirk party out of food and prevent — or at least delay — their arrival at Fort William.

McKenzie had retired two years previously after a stormy relationship with Nor'West management. For example, in 1809 McKenzie had complained to Duncan Cameron about "our worthy directors," saying, "... their plan is to get rid of their old experienced ... partners to make room for froth, pomp and ostentation."

Shortly after the battle, McKenzie visited his son Roderick, who was at Seven Oaks. When Roderick asked his father if they had done the right thing in going against the settlers, Daniel said that they had to defend themselves. Upon his return to Fort William, Daniel wrote to Roderick that the partners had been pleased with his (Roderick's) conduct at the Red River.

Up to this point Selkirk's actions at Fort William had all been according to the law. However, some of his actions after the arrested Nor'West partners left for Canada were certainly dubious. He had McKenzie thrown into jail, where conditions were appalling. One of the men imprisoned at Fort William after Seven Oaks (John Bourke) testified that the jail "... had been used as a privy, in which light was not admitted, except through crevices between the logs, of which the building was constructed, and in which an intolerable stench prevailed."

The guards plied McKenzie, who was reputed to be a drunkard, with liquor. After two days in jail, McKenzie agreed to cooperate, and Selkirk released him. Then, in a letter dated September 3, 1816, McKenzie testified about the Nor'West actions towards the Red River Settlement over the previous two years. He argued that he could act on the company's behalf because he was the only partner left at Fort William. He further claimed that the NWC owed him money.

McKenzie testified that after the Nor'West pemmican was seized by order of Captain Miles Macdonell in the summer of 1814, McGillivray ordered that presents of provisions and liquor be given to the people from Red River who were at Fort William. In addition, a gift of 60 pounds was to be sent to Mrs. McLean at the Red River, "as she was friendly and wished well to the North-West Company." McKenzie objected because the Nor'West partners had to help pay for

A view of the Red River Settlement in 1817,
thought to be from a sketch by Lord Selkirk

these gifts. "I know, however, that the presents were sent, and I believe they charged me with my share."

McKenzie also said that in the summer of 1815 the Nor'West partners gave many of the Métis presents of guns, swords, or daggers for their service against the Red River. He mentioned specifically that Bostonnais Pangman and Antoine Hoole each got a sword.

McKenzie concluded by saying that many of his fellow-Nor'Westers suspected him "of turning informer." One of these men, as he departed for Montreal under arrest, threatened McKenzie. He said, "If ever I am acquitted, I'll blow out your brains." This man, a relative of McKenzie's, drowned on the trip to Montreal.

Selkirk then arranged to buy all the moveable property in the fort from McKenzie, on condition that £60,000 worth of furs be kept in trust, along with one of Selkirk's Scottish estates worth £2,000 in annual rent. The transaction was to be referred to arbitrators in London. Selkirk later admitted that entering into this agreement had been "ill-judged."

John Pritchard, who arrived at Fort William shortly after McKenzie made his statement, later testified that McKenzie considered his business arrangement with Selkirk "advantageous to himself and the other wintering partners." McKenzie wanted to go to the Red River, where he "might be serviceable from his influence with the Half-Breeds," but he agreed to go to Montreal because Selkirk told him his testimony was very important.

Pritchard was also going to Montreal to testify, so he and McKenzie travelled together in a brigade of three canoes manned by Nor'West servants who were returning home. McKenzie was not under restraint during the trip but went as a voluntary witness.

However, at Sault Ste. Marie, McKenzie met some other Nor'Westers who convinced him to recant his testimony of September 3. McKenzie then formally protested the treatment he had received from Selkirk and swore before a notary that his testimony had been "a tissue of lies" mostly dictated by Miles Macdonell. He further charged that Macdonell and the de Meuron officers had kept him "in a state of inebriation and actual derangement of the mind."

On November 12, 1816, a Constable Robinson arrived at Fort William with the warrant McGillivray had obtained for Selkirk's arrest on charges of forcible entry and detention. Selkirk refused to obey the warrant, saying he would never yield the fort to anyone but the King's soldiers.

Selkirk's decision may have been influenced by news of the murder of Owen Keveny, leader of the group of 1812 Irish Selkirk settlers. Keveny had volunteered in the spring of 1816 to lead a force to the Red River to restore the settlement that had been destroyed the previous summer. He was evidently unaware that Colin Robertson had already restored it. According to later testimony, the six men who accompanied Keveny hated him because he treated them so harshly. Five of these men deserted Keveny near Lac-du-Bonnet on the Winnipeg River and made their way to Fort Bas-de-la-Rivière. They testified to the Nor'Wester in charge that Keveny had stabbed one man in the leg and shot another with a gun full of powder — in both cases because the men fell asleep from exhaustion.

The Nor'Westers arrested Keveny and planned to send him in chains to Fort William. Instead, after learning that Selkirk had seized Fort William, they abandoned Keveny on an island in the Winnipeg River. Shortly after, another party of Nor'Westers arrived on the island and murdered Keveny.

After Selkirk refused to obey the first warrant for his arrest, a second one was sent out with a deputy sheriff named William Smith. Smith did not reach Fort William until the following March (1817). When Smith tried to serve the warrant and arrest Selkirk, he was thrown into jail for nearly two months. Selkirk left for the Red River on May 1, and about a month later William McGillivray repossessed Fort William.

Two other events damaged Selkirk's image as a disinterested colonizer and weakened his case against the NWC. First, in the winter of 1816 Selkirk published a book that strongly attacked the NWC. Second, the HBC had authorized Selkirk to open secret negotiations with the NWC (conducted through a third party) regarding the amalgamation of the two fur trading companies. At this point, the Nor'Westers began to refer to Selkirk as "The Trading Lord."

Pierre Falcon wrote a ballad commemorating Selkirk's attempts to win the Métis away from the Nor'Westers during the winter he spent at Fort William.

### *Lord Selkirk at Fort William*

*Come quickly, come today*
*Rats-musqués [muskrats], Bois-Brûlés,*
*At Fort William Lord Selkirk gives a ball.*

*Now hurry, don't delay,*
*You'll sing and dance and play,*
*The band strikes up; there's food and fun for all.*

..........................

*The Battle of Seven Oaks*

*There see the drink flow free,*
*You'll dance abandonedly.*
*The band strikes up; there's food and fun for all.*

*Meurons, without delay,*
*Please play us something gay.*
*A lively tune to start our happy ball.*

*My Lord, we now express*
*Our thanks for your kindness.*
*When can we traders give you such a ball?*

# Chapter 9
# "Silver Chief" Reorganizes the Settlement

### Red River Settlement, 1817

In the fall of 1816, Selkirk had sent Miles Macdonell and a force of about 35 de Meurons from Fort William to retake Fort Douglas. It is unclear who Selkirk expected to command the expedition — Macdonell or the de Meurons's captain, Proteus D'Orsonnens. They were guided by John Tanner, a white American who had been kidnapped by the Shawnees at the age of nine and brought to the Red River country about four years later. Both Macdonell and Tanner wrote accounts of the expedition.

Macdonell later complained that, although he had "planned and executed" the expedition, "the chief merit of it was given afterwards to Capt. D'Orsonnens." He said that D'Orsonnens, due to "his want of knowledge of the habits of the country and the natives could no more execute it than he could fly. The de Meuron soldiers were well aware of this and refused to advance with him till after I had joined them."

John Tanner had reluctantly agreed to guide the force after Macdonell spent several days convincing him that the HBC "was acting with the sanction of the British government." Macdonell also promised to help Tanner return to the States and to give him "liberal presents, good treatment, and fair promises."

Tanner's report states that they had some hunters with them and great quantities of wild rice, so they "were pretty well supplied with food," although they had a long way to travel and the snow was deep. They ran out of meat on occasion, he said, and then there was occasionally "something of a mutinous disposition manifest among the soldiers, but little serious difficulty occurred."

The force began their expedition by seizing five horses, four cattle, and two oxen from the Nor'West fort at Rainy Lake. They reached Pembina on New Year's Eve. By this time, about 25 Natives had joined them, and they easily took Fort Daer.

This is how Macdonell described the final stage of their trip from Fort Daer to Fort Douglas. January 9 was a miserable day. The men had difficulty making headway against the cold northwest wind and drifting snow and finally had to stop and make a fire to warm themselves, as some were suffering frostbite. By sunset they had reached The Passage, a traditional place to cross the Assiniboine River, some 15 to 18 kilometres from Fort Douglas. This is the same place where Grant had been unable to leave the river on his way to Seven Oaks.

They were met at The Passage by Chief Peguis and nine of his followers. "Peguis," Macdonell wrote, "made me a present of 10 buffalo tongues, which were very acceptable having nothing for ourselves or men to eat." They decided to remain sheltered in the woods until midnight and then proceed to Fort Douglas before daylight. Macdonell gave the men each a little brandy, "which cheered them much," and they "set out in high spirits, certain of success." By this time the storm had abated, and it was not quite so cold. When they reached The Forks, sentries were placed outside the homes of each of the freemen living nearby to prevent the inhabitants from warning the Nor'Westers at Fort Douglas. The remaining men proceeded to Fort Douglas, where they prepared four ladders and placed them against the fort's outer walls.

According to Tanner's version, they met Chief Peguis with 12 men on the Assiniboine River. Macdonell, who "seemed at a loss" to know how to proceed, consulted with Peguis, who "advised them to march immediately up to the fort, and show their force before it, which he thought would be sufficient to ensure immediate surrender."

Tanner wrote that he was "dissatisfied." Macdonell and Peguis "took no notice of me in these consultations," he said. At any rate they finally decided to take the fort by surprise under cover of night. Tanner described the ladders that Macdonell mentioned, saying they were made "in the way the Indians make them, by cutting the trunk of a tree, with the limbs trimmed long enough to serve to step on, and placing it against the wall." He said the first men over the wall landed on the roof of the blacksmith's shop.

Some half dozen men climbed over the walls and opened the main gate for the rest of the force. By sunrise they had taken everyone inside prisoner and had raised their flag. Macdonell sent a party to Jack River to tell the settlers that Fort Douglas had been retaken and that Selkirk was coming to the Red River in the summer. A few of the settlers immediately returned to The Forks over the frozen Lake Winnipeg so they could rebuild houses and plant crops as soon as it was warm enough. The remaining settlers followed when the lake and rivers were free of ice. For some of them, it would be their third attempt in five years to build a home and start a farm. Sheriff Alexander Macdonell would remain as leader of the colony for the next couple of years.

Having heard about the recapture of Fort Douglas, Cuthbert Grant returned from Qu'Appelle with a group of followers who camped nearby, along the Assiniboine River. Grant and Miles Macdonell exchanged a few letters and insults, but no blows. Grant complained that the prisoners taken when Fort Douglas was recaptured were not treated well, and threatened "consequences" if their treatment was not improved.

Macdonell denied the accusation and said, "As to the threat you make, I despise it ... Your people are assembled unlawfully. I order you in His Majesty's name to disperse them and if after eight o'clock tomorrow morning you are found together in arms, I shall put the Riot Act in force and you must take the consequences."

Grant replied in like vein: "Your threats you make use of, we laugh at them and you may come with your forces at any time you please."

Selkirk arrived at the Red River on June 21, 1817, the day after his forty-sixth birthday. The arrival of the man the settlers could either thank or blame for bringing them to North America created great excitement. Selkirk was a tall, thin man who looked very frail due to the tuberculosis that would ultimately end his life.

Selkirk cancelled the land debts of the settlers who had suffered the loss of their farm improvements, so approximately 24 families now owned their farms debt-free. The remainder received land at five shillings per acre, which they would pay in produce to the HBC, according to the original agreement they had signed. Selkirk also set aside land for churches and schools. He suggested calling the district Kildonan, the name of the parish that many of the Scottish settlers had come from. He confirmed Peter Fidler's land survey. He also promised to have more cattle sent to the settlement and to try to find an experienced bricklayer and workers to build a gristmill and sawmill.

As well, Selkirk assured the Lagimodières that he had spoken to the Bishop of Quebec who had promised to send missionaries the following summer. This was in response to a request Jean-Baptiste Lagimodière had made when he agreed to deliver Colin Robertson's message to Selkirk in Montreal in the spring of 1816. "I ask you to give us Catholic missionaries," he had replied when Selkirk asked him what he would like as a reward. "I love the Red River, but since my wife is Canadian she wishes to come back to this country so that our children will not lose their religion."

Thus, it happened that, although neither Selkirk nor most of the settlers were Catholic, Selkirk gave the Catholic Church a large land grant at the Red River. He hoped the presence of this church would help to re-establish peace and keep the Métis in the settlement (as their Canadian fathers were mostly Catholics).

Selkirk also gave Lagimodière a grant of land at the junction of the Red and Seine Rivers. Most of the French, Métis, and Swiss people settled on the east side of the Red River and along the Seine River, while the people Selkirk had brought from Scotland and Ireland settled mainly on the west side of the Red River.

Another important item of business for Selkirk was the signing of treaties with five local Native chiefs, including Peguis. (The chiefs gave Selkirk the name "Silver Chief," likely because his hair was turning grey.)

Under these treaties the tribes gave up a two-mile-wide

strip of land on each side of the Red and Assiniboine Rivers. The strip along the Red River ran from Lake Winnipeg south into North Dakota. The Assiniboine strip ran westward from The Forks to a point beyond Portage la Prairie. In addition, two circles, each six miles in radius, were ceded around Fort Douglas and Fort Daer. To explain two miles to the Native people, Selkirk's men said the distance was "as far as a man can see under the belly of a horse on a clear day." In exchange for the land, each tribe was to receive a yearly payment of 100 pounds of "good merchantable" tobacco.

Peguis received a testimonial from Lord Selkirk stating that he was "one of the principal chiefs of the ... Saulteaux of Red River, has been a steady friend of the settlement ever since its first establishment, and has never deserted its cause in its greatest reverses." Also, Selkirk was able to put John Tanner in touch with his American family, and to give him a small pension in return for his help in recapturing Fort Douglas.

Selkirk remained at the Red River for less than three months before travelling back to the Canadas.

# Chapter 10
# Selkirk versus the Nor'Westers

**Red River Settlement, 1817–1818**

Lord Selkirk was not the only official visitor to the Red River during the summer of 1817. William Coltman, who arrived two weeks after Selkirk, visited in his capacity as the head of the commission to inquire into the events surrounding Seven Oaks.

The choice of Coltman as commissioner raised alarm bells for Selkirk and his supporters on several counts. Coltman was from Montreal, a city closely connected with the NWC, and he and McGillivray were acquaintances. Moreover, Coltman had travelled west with the Nor'West brigade

Coltman was described as "a good-natured, laugh-and-grow-fat sort of person who had no wish but to reconcile and tranquilize all parties." Although Selkirk's supporters considered this approach unjust, Lady Selkirk later acknowledged, "Such is the man's bonhomie and good nature that none of us can quite attribute bad intentions to him."

After consulting with both McGillivray and Selkirk, Coltman suggested a three-part compromise solution. The NWC would retire entirely from the Red River, the HBC would leave the Athabasca area solely to the Nor'Westers, and both sides would drop all charges before the courts. McGillivray was willing to consider the idea, but Selkirk completely rejected it.

Coltman worked 12-hour days during his stay at the Red River. He interviewed as many of the people connected with Seven Oaks as possible before returning to Lower Canada in the fall. He first interviewed Selkirk, whom he arrested and then freed on the exceedingly high bail of £6,000. Selkirk, who by this time was seriously ill with tuberculosis, left for London late in 1818 without waiting for the trials to be completed.

Next to Selkirk, the most important person Coltman had to deal with was Cuthbert Grant. As leader of the Métis, Grant was the person most likely to be able to restore peace at Red River and keep his followers from abandoning both the HBC and the NWC. Some of the Métis had already gone to trade with the Americans, and more were talking of doing so. Coltman wrote to Grant, asking him to surrender and go to Montreal so his conduct could be investigated. Coltman said he considered the murders of Owen Keveny and of those dispatched in cold blood at Seven Oaks very serious offences.

He also said, however, that "as for the battle itself, it is always understood that the colony people ... fired the first shot while Boucher was speaking to them. I consider this affair, as well as the other violent deeds which took place, although as serious offences against the law, yet such as may be pardoned."

Grant responded by riding to Coltman's camp to make his deposition. He then left for Canada with Coltman, travelling as a guest of the commissioner rather than a prisoner. Selkirk's people were not happy about that. Grant spent at least part of the winter in jail in Montreal; and a true bill was returned against him in February 1818 on six charges, including the murder of Owen Keveny. He was tried and acquitted of murdering Keveny. He next ought to have stood trial for the murder of Robert Semple, but he jumped bail and fled to the northwest by canoe.

Selkirk bitterly wrote that Grant was a "notorious criminal" who had been allowed to go untried and unpunished. François-Firmin Boucher did stand trial for Semple's murder, and was acquitted. The acquittal created the assumption that if Boucher was innocent, Grant was also. The charges against Grant were quietly shelved.

Charles Bottineau, a freeman hunter employed by the Nor'Westers, also made a deposition before Coltman. Bottineau stated that Duncan Cameron and Alexander Macdonell had issued an order to all the free Canadians in the Red River region late in 1814 prohibiting them from giving any food to the colonists or helping them in any manner — even if they were dying of starvation. Bottineau said that one freeman who dared to give food to the English was severely punished. The NWC seized his four horses and forced him to abandon his family and return to Montreal. The Nor'Westers also ordered Bottineau to drive away any animals that came near the settlement, and they promised to replace any of Bottineau's horses that were killed. Finally, Bottineau testified that in the summer of 1815, Cameron ordered him to burn the HBC fort at Pembina, but he refused to do so.

On June 30, 1818, almost one year after his visit to the Red River, Coltman submitted his report. He said he had doubts about the legal basis for the establishment of the Red River Settlement and Selkirk's actions at Fort William. On the other hand, while condemning both sides for their recourse to violence, he particularly denounced "the system of intimidation and violence" employed by the NWC. He also acknowledged that Selkirk sincerely believed the NWC was behaving as an enemy of both the government and the settlement. Selkirk could thus be excused for taking some actions that otherwise would have been unjustifiable. Coltman concluded that the Red River Settlement had not experienced criminal acts by individuals but rather incidents in a "private war" between two trading empires.

Coltman said the first shot at Seven Oaks was "next to a certainty" fired by Semple's party and that Grant had tried to prevent the savagery that ensued. "The total absence of any accusation against Grant on this score [of savagery] and the numerous testimonies to his general humanity, leave little doubt of the truth of this assertion," Coltman wrote.

Coltman described Nor'Wester Alexander Macdonell's words and actions as "general violence." Despite the many allegations against him, however, Macdonell was allowed to return to the west in 1817 without being tried in any court of law.

One of the charges against Alexander Macdonell was that he was responsible for the murder of Owen Keveny, but Macdonell maintained that two men named Mainville and de Reinhard had acted on their own initiative. Mainville escaped while being brought to Canada for trial. Charles de Reinhard, a former de Meuron sergeant and current NWC employee, confessed to the murder and was sentenced to be hanged.

All told, Selkirk laid 150 charges against the Nor'Westers and their allies, including 42 charges of murder and 19 of arson. Of all these charges, only the one against de Reinhard resulted in a guilty verdict. That sentence was not carried out, however, because of disputes over the exact location of the crime and the jurisdiction of the court. McGillivray and other Nor'Westers, in their turn, laid 29 charges against Selkirk and his supporters.

According to Coltman's report, the HBC and settlers lost so many men because they were "standing together in a crowd, unaccustomed to the use of fire-arms or any of the practices of irregular warfare." The Métis, on the other hand, were "excellent marksmen, advantageously posted in superior numbers around their opponents and accustomed as huntsmen, and from the habits of Indian warfare, to every device that could tend to their own preservation, or to the destruction of their enemy." Coltman also concluded that most of those involved at Seven Oaks were not responsible for the mutilation of bodies. He named only a French Canadian, François Deschamps, and his three sons as responsible. There is no indication why the Deschamps were not brought to trial.

Colin Robertson, who had left the Red River shortly before the Seven Oaks incident, had planned to sail for England in October. However, the ship became icebound and he was forced to winter in the North. In March 1817, he learned that the NWC had charged him for seizing Fort Gibraltar, so he travelled to Montreal to clear his name. He refused to accept bail and insisted on going to prison. He was acquitted in the spring of 1818.

John Pritchard testified at Colin Robertson's trial and then went to York (Toronto) as a witness at the trial of the two Nor'Westers charged in the murder of Robert Semple. Following the second trial, Pritchard travelled to London, where he presented a petition to the British Parliament, requesting protection for the Red River Settlement.

Selkirk was represented by his lawyer in two civil actions in the spring of 1819. Both were for false imprisonment at Fort William. In the first case, Daniel McKenzie charged that he was held in the "Black Hole" where his addiction to alcohol was exploited and he was induced to sell Fort William and much of its goods to Selkirk. McKenzie was awarded damages of £1,500. The second case was brought by Deputy Sheriff William Smith, who had been held in jail for almost two months after he attempted to arrest Selkirk in the spring of 1817. Smith received damages of £500. Thus, although a number of people involved in Seven Oaks spent a short time in jail, Selkirk was the only person who actually paid a court-imposed penalty.

As a direct result of the Coltman Commission report, in 1821 the British Parliament passed "An Act for Regulating the Fur Trade and Establishing a Criminal and Civil Jurisdiction within Certain Parts of North America." The Act stated that the provisions of the Canada Jurisdiction Act of 1803 were to extend throughout all of the Hudson Bay territories. It gave the courts in Upper Canada the same civil and criminal jurisdiction within the "Indian territories" as they had within Upper Canada. Justices of the peace authorized to try criminal and civil cases were to be appointed for the Indian territories. Only cases subject to capital punishment or civil cases involving sums over £200 had to be tried in Upper Canada.

# Chapter 11
# Facing Flood and Famine

**Red River Settlement, 1818–1834**

John McLeod, leader of the men who refused to surrender when the settlement was destroyed in 1815, arrived back at The Forks in the summer of 1818. He was in charge of a large brigade that included a group of 40 French-Canadian settlers and the Catholic missionaries that Selkirk had promised. Everyone was amazed when Reverend Joseph-Norbert Provencher stepped out of the canoe wearing his long, black robe. At 6 feet 4 inches, Provencher was almost a foot taller than most of the voyageurs. He quickly became known as the "Giant of the West."

Because grasshoppers had infested the settlement, the French-Canadian settlers barely paused before continuing on to Pembina. That year, the grasshoppers hadn't arrived until early August, when the wheat was sufficiently far along to escape major damage. However, the following year the grasshoppers arrived in May, and destroyed all the grain and even the prairie grass needed to feed the cattle and horses. The grasshoppers lay on the ground to a depth of two to four inches and were especially bad near sources of water. One of the settlers later wrote, "Along the river they were to be found in heaps, like seaweed, and might be shovelled with a spade ... Every green substance was eaten up or stripped to the bare stalk ... leaving no hope of either seed to the sower or bread to the eater."

By 1820, the grasshoppers had subsided and the crops looked promising, but that year field mice did as much damage as the grasshoppers had in other years. By now, the settlers had run out of seed grain. Someone went to buy grain at Dog Plain on the Mississippi in the spring of 1821, only to arrive back too late for the seed to be planted that season.

Sheriff Alexander Macdonell remained in charge of the settlement until 1822 (when he was replaced by Andrew Bulger). For the first few years, the settlers were satisfied with the sheriff's leadership, although some of the HBC officers criticized his management and implied that he was dishonest. According to Colin Robertson, the HBC people were critical because Macdonell prevented them from overcharging the settlers for supplies. The settlers even sent a petition to Selkirk in support of Macdonell, in August 1819.

Following Sheriff Macdonell's return from a trip to

Scotland over the winter of 1819–1820, however, the settlers also began to complain about him. Macdonell was accused of almost every possible wrongdoing — financial dishonesty, nepotism, encouraging dissension among colony officials, drunkenness, and immorality. Macdonell became known as the "Grasshopper Governor" because "he proved as great a destroyer within doors as the grasshoppers in the fields."

In September 1821, HBC Governor Simpson began to investigate these complaints. He found them valid and had Macdonell dismissed in March 1822. Macdonell remained in the settlement as a farmer until finally leaving for Upper Canada in 1828.

John Pritchard wrote an interesting report about the cost of living at the Red River in 1819. Strangely, the family Pritchard used as an example consisted of only a couple (whom he assumed "to be inactive") and their two servants. It is unlikely that anyone prosperous enough to hire servants would have come to the Red River. Moreover, Pritchard made no mention of children — in a population that consisted largely of people under the age of 40.

Pritchard calculated that when the couple arrived they would require £20 to hire two men for three months to build a house, £30 "to finish and furnish" the house, and £10 to purchase a team of horses and harness. Yearly necessities would include a fish net and 100 fish hooks, four pounds each of gunpowder and shot, six buffalo for meat, £35 for servants' wages, £30 for "suitable clothing for a gentleman and lady," and such miscellaneous items as tea and sugar. A person would require £457.96 (roughly equivalent to over $1,000 CDN in 2002) to purchase the items that cost Pritchard £10 in 1820.

Pritchard said the remainder of necessities were available with some labour. The fishing gear and ammunition would "procure as much fish, waterfowl and other birds as the family will require." Even in the first year, the manservant would be able to raise "sufficient wheat and culinary articles" to support the family and pay for his tools. Finally, a good housewife could brew ale, make wines from the abundant wild fruit, make sugar from the sap of the maple tree, and make soap and candles from buffalo fat.

No more large groups of settlers came from Scotland after 1815. The Swiss de Meuron settler-soldiers who arrived with Selkirk included at least 10 Polish soldiers who had also served in the de Meuron regiment. Selkirk had hoped to recruit a large number of Polish settlers, but his plans came to nothing.

In the Scots' opinion, the Swiss and Polish settlers were lazy, deceitful, and "a rough and lawless set of blackguards." Since Selkirk had taken great care in selecting the de Meuron veterans, choosing "none but those of the best character and who knew some of the requisite and useful trades for settlement," the Scots' attitudes undoubtedly arose from racial and religious prejudices. The Swiss and Polish settlers were likely as capable and of as good character as the Scots.

More Swiss settlers arrived in 1821, bringing with them

a number of marriageable young women. Eight days after the group arrived, 10 Swiss girls had already married local men. By the fall of 1819, there were 88 houses in the settlement with 10 more under construction. By 1822, the population stood at 681, with three men for every two women.

While many Swiss girls married fur traders, there was little intermarriage between the Scottish women and the fur traders.

In 1820, the first Anglican (Church of England) missionary, Reverend John West, arrived under the auspices of the Church Missionary Society of England and the HBC. West was not favourably impressed with his first view of the settlement. He wrote that it consisted "of a number of huts widely scattered along the margin of the river. In vain did I look for a cluster of cottages ... as in a village. I saw but few marks of human industry in the cultivation of the soil. Almost every inhabitant we passed bore a gun upon his shoulder and all appeared in a wild and hunter-like state."

Before returning to England in 1823, West had erected a school and a church at the Red River, but most of the Scottish settlers were Presbyterians. As one of them said, "The Church of England minister was there without a congregation while the Scots had a congregation without a minister." Although Selkirk had promised a Gaelic-speaking Presbyterian minister and had set aside land for the church in 1817, for some unknown reason, the first Presbyterian church was not built until 1851.

By 1822, the Red River had a library of reference books, poetry, and a few novels, such as *Don Quixote* and *Robinson Crusoe*. That same year, Peter Fidler died and left the settlement his library of "all my printed books amounting to about 500 volumes," two sets of 12-inch globes, a large telescope, a microscope, a brass sextant, and a barometer.

The Red River Settlement was left in relative peace following Coltman's investigation, but the HBC and Nor'Westers continued their struggle for fur trade supremacy until they were officially united under the HBC name on March 26, 1821. Selkirk did not live to see that day.

Shortly before Selkirk's death in France in April 1820, the NWC offered to buy his HBC stocks. He might have been tempted to accept the offer, since by now he was in serious financial difficulty. He had suffered direct losses when the settlement was destroyed and had incurred expenses for his legal battle. Nonetheless, he refused. He wrote:

> With respect to giving up the settlement or selling it to the North West Company, that is entirely out of the question ... I ground this resolution, not only on the principle of supporting the settlers whom I have already sent to the place, but also because I consider my character at stake upon the success of the undertaking, and upon proving it was neither a wild or visionary scheme nor a cloak to cover sordid plans of aggression, charges which

would be left in too ambiguous a state if I were to abandon the settlement ... and above all if I were to sell it to its enemies.

The settlers, hearing about Selkirk's death, feared they would lose everything. Two years later, in the summer of 1822, Selkirk's brother-in-law, John Halkett, visited the Red River to reassure the settlers that Selkirk's death made no difference to their status. Halkett also dealt with some of the settlers' grievances, including their concerns about being overcharged for goods because they were forced to purchase everything through the HBC. Halkett succeeded in reducing the prices of goods and the interest rates for loans.

The British government named Andrew Bulger as Governor of Assiniboia in 1822, and he arrived just in time to meet with Halkett. The first formal meeting of the Council of Assiniboia took place on December 24, 1822. John Pritchard was one of the four council members.

Almost immediately, Governor Bulger and the chief factor of the HBC came into conflict, as the division of authority between the two was not clearly defined. Bulger resigned, and by the time his replacement arrived, the British government had decided that the HBC factor would outrank the governor.

At this time, the International Boundary Line between the United States and the British or Hudson's Bay Company territory was set at the 49th parallel. An 1823 survey determined that Pembina was on the American side of the border.

The HBC, wishing to keep the Métis as part of the Red River Settlement, gave Cuthbert Grant a piece of land on the Assiniboine River at White Horse Plains in 1824. There, with a group of about 100 Métis families, Grant founded the community of Grantown (later known as St. François Xavier). In 1828, the HBC appointed Grant as "Warden of the Plains" to prevent illicit trade in furs in the area. For the next 20 years, he was at various times a justice of the peace, captain of the buffalo hunt, and councillor and sheriff of Assiniboia. In 1854, he died following a fall from his horse.

After a decade of constant struggle and near desperation, the settlers finally raised their first good crops in 1825 and 1826. At last they harvested enough potatoes and root vegetables for the winter and enough grain that bread could become a regular part of their diet. Although critics claimed the soil was poor, the main reason for the frequent crop failures was early frosts. This remained a problem until earlier-maturing wheat varieties were developed decades later.

Disaster soon returned, however. The winter of 1825–1826 was extremely cold, with an unusually large amount of snow. Although most of the settlers survived the hard winter, 33 hunters and their families perished on the nearby plains in a blizzard in late December. Spring brought relief from the cold, but it also resulted in the worst flood in living memory.

*Facing Flood and Famine*

John Pritchard described the flood in letters to his brother in England. He reported that the ice on the Red River broke up late one evening during the first week of May. "The night was dark and stormy, accompanied with rain. The flood at once rose higher than ever known by man. The crashing of immense masses of ice was loud as thunder; neither the tallest poplar nor the stoutest oak could resist its impetuosity. They were mowed down like grass before the scythe."

All the settlers and their cattle made for the nearest high land, gradually moving farther from the river as it continued to rise. Finally, those settlers living on the east side of the river took refuge on Birds Hill, while those living west of the river went to Stony Mountain. The approximately 25 kilometres of land between Birds Hill and Stony Mountain was covered with about 10 metres of water. The water continued to rise until the beginning of June. Then, as the water level gradually fell, the settlers slowly retraced their steps homeward. As soon as the soil was dry enough, they planted crops of potatoes, barley, and some wheat. Although no human lives were lost in the settlement and only a few cattle drowned, every building was destroyed except for the windmill and three churches. Only one bag of seed wheat that had been stored in a church bell tower remained, but neighbouring trading posts sent some seed. Because of the heat and the moisture, the crops grew so quickly that by August 21 Pritchard could write, "both wheat and barley are in full ear and the potatoes sufficiently large for the table."

Many settlers, including most of the de Meurons, were completely demoralized by the flood and left for the United States or Canada. A few returned to Europe. Others, like John Pritchard and Jean-Baptiste Lagimodière, were determined to remain no matter what happened. Those settlers who left were offset to some degree by the influx of Hudson Bay employees and their Native families. These men had served their contracted time with the HBC or had been thrown out of work when the two fur trading companies amalgamated. The 1832 census reported 2,457 people living along the Red River and 294 at Grantown on the Assiniboine with 445 houses in total. By this time, there were at least four schools and several small flour mills in the settlement.

In 1834 the executors of Lord Selkirk's estate reconveyed Assiniboia to the HBC for a payment of £84,000. At that time £1,000 had approximately the same purchasing power as £70,000 has today. Thus, the Selkirk estate received payment in today's funds of about $15 million CDN. Although the settlers' rights to land they had purchased or received as grants was not affected, the authorities transferred the land back to the HBC without consulting or even informing the settlers.

One report says that Selkirk expended £85,000 on the Red River Settlement, three times as much as the colony would have brought if put up for auction. In addition to the losses suffered at the hands of the Nor'Westers, the settlement experienced a number of expensive business failures such as Selkirk's unsuccessful attempts to introduce Merino sheep into the country and to establish three separate experimental farms.

In 1833, after more than 20 years of struggle, Governor Donald MacKenzie reported enthusiastically that the Red River Settlement was "going most thrivingly forward" with "large and flourishing harvests" and healthy and contented people. While MacKenzie was almost certainly exaggerating, the settlement had survived its difficult birth and emerged as an adult.

# Epilogue

In 1891, to mark the 75th anniversary of Seven Oaks, Selkirk's daughter-in-law unveiled a monument in Winnipeg with this inscription:

> Erected ... by the Manitoba Historical Society, through the generosity of the Countess of Selkirk on the Site of Seven Oaks, where fell Governor Robert Semple and twenty of his officers and men, June 19th, 1816.

Although the events at Seven Oaks occurred nearly 200 years ago, they continue to raise strong emotions among the descendants of the people involved. For many Métis, for example, Seven Oaks is the historic moment when their people first stood up for their rights as a nation against England and the Hudson's Bay Company. They are concerned that some historians still portray the Métis as aggressors and describe the battle as a massacre. They would prefer to call it a "skirmish" or "confrontation."

Some descendents of the Red River settlers feel equally strongly that "massacre" is the only appropriate term. The president of the Lord Selkirk Society was absolutely furious with an historian who used the word "battle" in an address to the Manitoba Historical Society circa 1970. She confronted him after his speech, eyes blazing. "You know it wasn't a battle ...," she said. "You know it was a massacre ... how could you have called it a battle?"

Grant MacEwan said he wrote *Cornerstone Colony: Selkirk's Contribution to the Canadian West* "with a conviction that the Red River Settlement in its first 25 troubled years made a deeper and more lasting imprint on what was to become Western Canada than the fur trade made in 200 years. The colony should be presented as the cornerstone upon which western agriculture in all its enduring greatness was founded."

In view of the current state of Canadian agriculture, people may question MacEwan's view. Not only has farm income dropped significantly in recent years, but also the percentage of the Canadian population engaged in farming fell from 75 per cent in 1867 to under 2 per cent in 2001.

Several of the leading participants in the early events at the Red River Settlement soon left the country. They included William Auld, Miles Macdonell, the two Alexander Macdonells, Colin Robertson, and Duncan Cameron.

Auld, who had been in charge at York Factory when the first settlers arrived, resigned from the HBC in 1815 and spent the last 15 years of his life in his native Scotland.

Miles Macdonell never returned to the northwest after going to Montreal for the trials following the battle of Seven Oaks. He lived in semi-retirement until his death in 1828, spending much of his time in an unsuccessful attempt to recover money he believed Selkirk owed him. There can be little argument that Macdonell's significant character faults and frequently poor judgment were the source of many of the problems at the settlement during his time as its leader.

Nor'Wester Alexander Macdonell, Miles's cousin, lost his position following the amalgamation of the HBC and the NWC in 1821. He returned to Upper Canada where he entered politics. Like Selkirk, he died of tuberculosis.

Colin Robertson became a chief factor in 1821, but his career was not successful because he and HBC Governor George Simpson did not get along. In 1832 he suffered a stroke and finally retired to Lower Canada in 1840. He died early in 1842 after being thrown from his sleigh in an accident.

Nor'Wester Duncan Cameron, who had been arrested by Colin Robertson in March 1816, spent a year in detention at York Factory before being sent to England. There he was released without standing trial, and he returned to North America about 1820. He took legal action against Robertson for false imprisonment (apparently unsuccessfully), requesting "damages to an enormous amount." Cameron then retired to Glengarry County in Upper Canada.

What of the people who lived out their lives in the northwest?

Pierre Falcon continued to work as a fur trader until 1824, when he became one of the first people to take up land at Grantown. He was named a justice of the peace for the settlement and continued to compose songs and poetry for the rest of his life, including one about the Red River Resistance of 1869–1870.

Jean-Baptiste and Marie-Anne (Gaboury) Lagimodière were the founders of one of the leading French Canadian/Métis families in the Red River. By 1886, they already had 632 direct descendants. Their grandson Louis Riel led the Red River Resistance in an attempt to negotiate more favourable terms from the Canadian government, when the Red River was transferred from the HBC to Canada and became part of the new Canadian province of Manitoba. Then, in 1885, Riel was executed for his role in the Northwest Rebellion.

Chief Peguis supported the missionary work of the Anglican Church and became a Christian in 1840. He had to give up three of his four wives in order to be baptized. He and his remaining wife took the names William and Victoria King. Peguis called himself King in recognition of his position in the tribe, and he is quoted as saying, "My sons are now princes and shall be known by that name." One of his great-great-grandsons, Tommy Prince, who fought in both World War II and the Korean War, became Canada's most-decorated Aboriginal war veteran

Chief Peguis received an annuity of £5 per year from Governor George Simpson in 1835. In later life, he became dissatisfied with the white settlers who began to occupy land that his tribe had not surrendered. He made a formal protest, saying the tobacco was merely a token payment and that formal surrender of the land had never taken place. He died in 1864, when he was about 90 years old, before his claim was settled.

John Pritchard became a leading citizen of the Red River Settlement. He was a fur trader, farmer, politician, school teacher and businessman over the course of his long life. He remained a member of the Council of Assiniboia until 1848 and died in 1856.

Pritchard's grandson, Reverend Canon Samuel Pritchard Matheson, spoke at the unveiling of the Seven Oaks Monument in 1891. He said, "My grandfather took part in the unfortunate conflict ... and was one of the few who survived that sad and fatal day ... He owed his life to the clemency and intercession of a friendly French Canadian ... [As] an adopted son in the home of that grandfather, I well remember what a close friendship was cherished and maintained to the relatives of the French Canadian for his kind deed ... I am thankful ... that a wise Providence overruled the disunion of that past, and so soon welded the discordant ... elements of those early days in a community of happy, contented and self-reliant people."

# Further Reading

Bryce, George and Charles Bell. "Seven Oaks," pp. 61–94. *A Thousand Miles of Prairie: The Manitoba Historical Society and the History of Western Canada*. Edited by Jim Blanchard. Winnipeg: University of Manitoba Press, 2002.

Coutts, Robert and Richard Stuart (eds.). *The Forks and the Battle of Seven Oaks in Manitoba History*. Winnipeg: Manitoba Historical Society, 1994.

Green, Wilson F. *Red River Revelations: A Chronological Account of Early Events Leading to the Discovery, Occupation, and Development of the Red River Settlement*. Winnipeg: Red River Valley International Centennial, 1974.

Hargrave, J. J. *Red River*. Published in Manitoba. 1st printing, 1871. 2nd printing 1977.

Healy, W. J. *Women of Red River: Being a book written from the recollections of women surviving from the Red River era*. Winnipeg: Women's Canadian Club, 1923. Reprinted with index, 1977.

MacEwan, Grant. *Cornerstone Colony: Selkirk's Contribution to the Canadian West.* Saskatoon: Western Producer Prairie Books, 1977.

MacEwan, Grant. *Métis Makers of History.* Saskatoon: Western Producer Prairie Books, 1981.

MacLeod, Margaret and W. L. Morton. *Cuthbert Grant of Grantown: Warden of the Plains of Red River.* Toronto: McClelland and Stewart, 1974.

Matheson, Samuel. "Floods at Red River," pp. 239–54. *A Thousand Miles of Prairie: The Manitoba Historical Society and the History of Western Canada.* Edited by Jim Blanchard. Winnipeg: University of Manitoba Press, 2002.

Morrison, Jean. *Superior Rendez-Vous Place: Fort William in the Canadian Fur Trade.* Toronto: Natural Heritage Books, 2001.

Morton, W. L. *Manitoba: A History.* 2nd edition. Toronto: University of Toronto Press, 1967. (Original edition, 1957.)

Rasky, Frank. *The Taming of the Canadian West.* Toronto: McClelland and Stewart, 1967.

## Further Reading

Stubbs, Roy St. George. *Four Recorders of Rupert's Land.* Winnipeg: Peguis Publishers, 1967.

Van Kirk, Sylvia. *"Many Tender Ties": Women in Fur-Trade Society, 1670–1870.* Winnipeg: Watson and Dwyer, 1980.

# List of Major Characters

**Leaders of Red River Settlement**

**Owen Keveny:** Irish leader of the second group of settlers, 1812

**Captain Miles Macdonell:** governor, 1811–1815

**Archibald Macdonald:** leader of the third group of settlers, 1814

**Colin Robertson:** re-established the settlement after it was destroyed in 1815

**Robert Semple:** governor, 1815–1816

**Sheriff John Spencer:** issued Pemmican Proclamation with Miles Macdonell in 1814

**Hudson's Bay Company Employees**

**William Auld:** Superintendent of Northern Department who met the first groups of settlers at York Factory

**Peter Fidler:** fur trader who surveyed the Red River Settlement and acted as a leader in the settlement from 1812 to 1817 (then returned to his previous position in charge of Brandon House)

**Pierre-Chrysologue Pambrun:** clerk captured by the Nor'Westers while delivering pemmican to Fort Douglas from Qu'Appelle before the Battle of Seven Oaks in 1816

**William Sinclair:** factor of Oxford House, 1789–1814

### Nor'Westers

**Duncan Cameron:** became a Nor'West partner in 1814; one of the leaders in the campaign to destroy the Red River Settlement

**Cuthbert Grant:** a clerk; named Captain-General of the Métis in 1816

**Alexander Macdonell:** became a Nor'West partner in 1814 and a leader against the settlers (cousin to Miles Macdonell)

**William McGillivray:** head of the NWC from 1804 until its merger with the HBC in 1821

**John Pritchard:** fur trader at the Red River from 1800 until he resigned from the NWC in 1814; then became a farmer and businessman in the Red River Settlement

**John Wills:** Cuthbert Grant's brother-in-law; in charge of Fort Gibraltar until his death in 1814

### Métis and Canadian Freemen

**Jean-Baptiste Lagimodière:** buffalo hunter who carried a message from the Red River to Selkirk in Montreal over the winter of 1815–1816

**Peter Pangman (Bostonnais):** buffalo hunter; stood trial for attacks against Red River Settlement and was acquitted

# List of Place Names

**Nor'West Forts**

**Fort Bas-de-la-Rivière:** on the Winnipeg River on the east side of Lake Winnipeg

**Fort Gibraltar:** at The Forks (of the Red and Assiniboine Rivers), now the centre of Winnipeg

**Fort La Souris:** on the Assiniboine River near its junction with the Souris River

**Fort Pembina:** at the junction of the Red and Pembina Rivers, on the American side of the present-day Manitoba-North Dakota border

**Fort L'Esperance:** on the Qu'Appelle River in eastern Saskatchewan

**Fort William:** on the northwest side of Lake Superior (now Thunder Bay)

**Hudson Bay Forts**

**Brandon House:** across from Fort La Souris on the Assiniboine River

**Fort Churchill:** on the southwestern side of Hudson Bay

**Fort Daer:** at Pembina, home of the settlers over the first winters at the Red River

**Fort Douglas:** near Fort Gibraltar and The Forks

**Jack River House:** at the north end of Lake Winnipeg, replaced by Norway House after 1814

**Qu'Appelle River Fort:** near the Nor'West Fort L'Esperance (It was referred to as the Hudson Bay's house and does not appear to have had another name.)

**York Factory:** on Hudson Bay near the junction of the Nelson and Hayes Rivers

# Acknowledgments

In addition to the books listed in Further Reading, the online resources of the Manitoba Historical Society and the *Dictionary of Canadian Biography Online* (which contains biographies of most of the characters in this book) were very useful.

# Photo Credits

**Cover:** Hudson Bay Company Archives; Provincial Archives of Manitoba: pages 8, 15; Hudson Bay Company Archives: page 20; National Archives of Canada: pages 65 (C-000624), 92 (C-008714).

# About the Author

Irene Gordon lives along the Assiniboine River in Headingley, Manitoba. She has had a passion for history and writing since childhood. After a career as a teacher-librarian, she became a freelance writer in 1998.

She enjoys reading and outdoor activities such as canoeing, hiking, skiing, sailing, swimming, and travelling. Above all, she enjoys spending time with her three young grandsons, Jesse, Riley, and Felix.

# Amazing Author
# Question and Answer

### What was your inspiration for writing about the Battle of Seven Oaks?

The establishment of the Red River Settlement by Lord Selkirk is one of the major events in early Manitoba history, and I already had some of the research done because of writing the *Amazing Stories* book about Marie-Anne Lagimodière.

### What surprised you most while you were researching the Battle of Seven Oaks?

I was most surprised at how hard the settlers' lives were. Some actually had to rebuild their homes three times in the space of five years.

### What do you most admire about Lord Selkirk?

Lord Selkirk can be admired for his desire to help the poor of Scotland and Ireland. His poor judgment in selecting people to lead the settlement, however, resulted in much unnecessary difficulty for the settlers.

### What escapade do you most identify with?

I can't say that I actually identify with any of them. The hardships the settlers underwent are almost beyond imagining for those of us living in Canada today.

## What difficulties did you run into when researching the Battle of Seven Oaks?

The establishment of the Red River Settlement is one of the most thoroughly documented events in Canadian history, so there was lots of material. The problem was that there were so many people and so many separate events involved that it was difficult to make the story clear and easy to follow.

## What part of the writing process did you enjoy most?

I most enjoy doing the research and writing the first complete draft of the book.

## Why did you become a writer? Who inspired you?

I have enjoyed writing and reading ever since I was a child. When I was 10 or 12, I read several children's novels based on Western Canadian history by a Manitoba woman named Olive Knox. You might say that she was a major inspiration — both for my interest in history and in writing.

## Who are your Canadian heroes?

Two would be Marie-Anne Lagimodière and Nellie McClung.

## by the same author

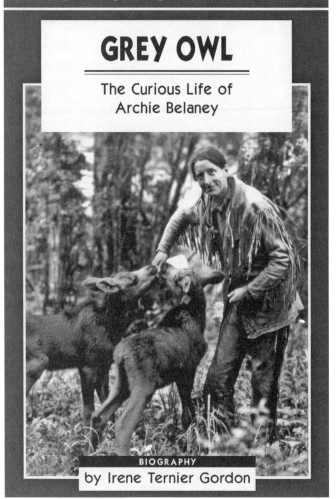

AMAZING STORIES™

# GREY OWL

The Curious Life of
Archie Belaney

BIOGRAPHY
by Irene Ternier Gordon

# GREY OWL
## The Curious Life of Archie Belaney

*"He gave his extraordinary genius, his passionate sympathy, his bodily strength, his magnetic personal influence, even his very earnings to the service of animals..."*
**Lovat Dickson, publisher**

Grey Owl was known to millions of people as an outstanding Native Canadian spokesman who championed the cause of nature, conservation, and preservation. His cause was true, but the truth about Archie Belaney's mysterious ancestry was another story.

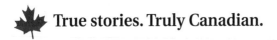 True stories. Truly Canadian.

ISBN 1-55153-785-0

AMAZING STORIES™

# MARIE-ANNE LAGIMODIÈRE

The Incredible Story of
Louis Riel's Grandmother

HISTORY/BIOGRAPHY

by Irene Ternier Gordon

# MARIE-ANNE LAGIMODIÈRE

## The Incredible Story of Louis Riel's Grandmother

*"Marie-Anne, seven months pregnant, would have to travel 50 kilometres on horseback. Unfazed, she set off with [a baby] hanging from one side of the saddle in her moss bag, balanced by a bag of provisions on the other side."*

Marie-Anne Lagimodière was a force to be reckoned with. Her honeymoon was a four-month journey from Quebec to Pembina with a brigade of tough voyageurs. She criss-crossed Canada with her fur trader husband during the early 1800s. Her legacy is enormous. Within 10 years of her death, at the ripe old age of 95, she already had more than 630 direct descendants including Louis Riel, the Métis leader.

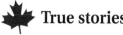 True stories. Truly Canadian.

ISBN 1-55153-967-5

AMAZING STORIES™

# THE INCREDIBLE ADVENTURES OF LOUIS RIEL

Canada's Most Famous Revolutionary

HISTORY/BIOGRAPHY

by Cat Klerks

# THE INCREDIBLE ADVENTURES OF LOUIS RIEL
## Canada's Most Famous Revolutionary

*"Fifteen years ago, I gave my heart to this nation, and I am ready to give it again."*
**Louis Riel, 1884**

Louis Riel is perhaps the most controversial figure in Canadian history. A rebel and a powerful orator, he emerged as a leader of the Métis in the Red River Settlement. His ability to unite the Métis nation was legendary. Although known as the Father of Manitoba, he spent much of his adult life in exile. He was found guilty of treason and hanged in Regina on 16 November, 1885.

 True stories. Truly Canadian.

ISBN 1-55153-955-1

# OTHER AMAZING STORIES

These titles are available wherever you buy books. If you have trouble finding the book you want, call the Altitude order desk at **1-800-957-6888**, e-mail your request to: **orderdesk@altitudepublishing.com** or visit our Web site **at www.amazingstories.ca**

New **AMAZING STORIES** titles are published every month.